INSIDE THE MINDS

Understanding Sports Law

Leading Lawyers on Navigating the Wide World of Sports Law: Contracts, Employment, Wealth Management, and Intellectual Property

ASPATORE

For additional copies or customer service inquiries, please e-mail west.customer.service@thomson.com.

ISBN 978-0-314-29252-0

Mat #41680665

Praise for *Inside the Minds*

"This series provides a practical and focused discussion of the leading issues in law today." – John V. Biernacki, Partner, Jones Day

"*Inside the Minds* draws from the collective experience of the best professionals. The books are informative from an academic, and, more importantly, practical perspective. I highly recommend them." – Keith M. Aurzada, Partner, Bryan Cave LLP

"Aspatore's *Inside the Minds* series provides practical, cutting edge advice from those with insight into the real world challenges that confront businesses in the global economy." – Michael Bednarek, Partner, Shearman & Sterling LLP

"What to read when you want to be in the know—topical, current, practical, and useful information on areas of the law that everyone is talking about." – Erika L. Morabito, Partner, Patton Boggs LLP

"Some of the best insight around from sources in the know" – Donald R. Kirk, Shareholder, Fowler White Boggs PA

"The *Inside the Minds* series provides a unique window into the strategic thinking of key players in business and law." – John M. Sylvester, Partner, K&L Gates LLP

"Comprehensive analysis and strategies you won't find anywhere else." – Stephen C. Stapleton, Of Counsel, Dykema Gossett PLLC

"The *Inside the Minds* series is a real hands-on, practical resource for cutting edge issues." – Trey Monsour, Partner, Haynes and Boone LLP

"A tremendous resource, amalgamating commentary from leading professionals that is presented in a concise, easy to read format." – Alan H. Aronson, Shareholder, Akerman Senterfitt

"Unique and invaluable opportunity to gain insight into the minds of experienced professionals." – Jura C. Zibas, Partner, Lewis Brisbois Bisgaard & Smith LLP

"A refreshing collection of strategic insights, not dreary commonplaces, from some of the best of the profession." – Roger J. Magnuson, Partner, Dorsey & Whitney LLP

"Provides valuable insights by experienced practitioners into practical and theoretical developments in today's ever-changing legal world." – Elizabeth Gray, Partner, Willkie, Farr & Gallagher LLP

"This series provides invaluable insight into the practical experiences of lawyers in the trenches." – Thomas H. Christopher, Partner, Kilpatrick Stockton LLP

ASPATORE

Aspatore Books, a Thomson Reuters business, exclusively publishes C-Level executives and partners from the world's most respected companies and law firms. Each publication provides professionals of all levels with proven business and legal intelligence from industry insiders—direct and unfiltered insight from those who know it best. Aspatore Books is committed to publishing an innovative line of business and legal titles that lay forth principles and offer insights that can have a direct financial impact on the reader's business objectives.

Each chapter in the *Inside the Minds* series offers thought leadership and expert analysis on an industry, profession, or topic, providing a future-oriented perspective and proven strategies for success. Each author has been selected based on their experience and C-Level standing within the business and legal communities. *Inside the Minds* was conceived to give a first-hand look into the leading minds of top business executives and lawyers worldwide, presenting an unprecedented collection of views on various industries and professions.

<u>CONTENTS</u>

Adisa P. Bakari **7**
Partner and Chair, The Sports Entertainment Group,
Kelley Drye & Warren LLP
THE EVOLUTION OF ATHLETE REPRESENTATION: THE GAME HAS CHANGED!

Donald Prophete **23**
***Shareholder,* Littler Mendelson**
EFFECTIVELY REPRESENTING SPORTS ORGANIZATIONS AND UNIVERSITIES

Travis J. Leach **43**
***Partner,* Ballard Spahr LLP**
THE WIDE WORLD OF SPORTS LAW: KEEPING UP WITH THE CORPORATE TAKEOVER OF SPORTS

Joseph Z. Fleming **57**
***Shareholder,* Greenberg Traurig PA**
RESPONDING TO RECENT SPORTS LAW TRENDS THROUGH INTERNAL SENSITIVITY TRAINING PROGRAMS

Alan Goudiss, *Partner,* and **75**
Christopher LaVigne, *Counsel*
Shearman & Sterling LLP
CONDUCTING AN EFFECTIVE SPORTS INVESTIGATION

Jill Haley Penwarden 95
***Partner,* Duane Morris LLP**
SPORTS LAW LITIGATION: RISK MANAGEMENT CONSIDERATIONS IN REPRESENTING RECREATION PROVIDERS AND DEFENSES TO SPORTS INJURY CLAIMS

Kelly Charles Crabb 111
***Partner,* Sheppard Mullin Richter & Hampton LLP**
LEGAL ISSUES SURROUNDING THE OLYMPIC GAMES AND OTHER SPORTING EVENTS ENTERING THE 21st CENTURY

Jonathan D. Goins 127
***Partner,* Lewis Brisbois Bisgaard & Smith LLP**
INTELLECTUAL PROPERTY RIGHTS IN IMAGE ADVERTISING

Appendices 137

The Evolution of Athlete Representation: The Game Has Changed!

Adisa P. Bakari

Partner and Chair, The Sports Entertainment Group

Kelley Drye & Warren LLP

ASPATORE

Introduction

My Dream Job

This is my dream job. Since the age of ten, the game of football has been instrumental to my life. Like most boys growing up playing youth and high school football, I dreamed of one day running out of the tunnel, on to the field of an NFL franchise. I quickly learned in college (and came to grips with about *three days* ago) that I would not be playing professionally the sport I so loved. By my junior year, I had concluded that making sure I had my academics ducks in a row, and thus ensuring a smooth transition to law school, was probably more worthy of my time than continuing my childhood dream. So, I hung up my proverbial cleats and started focusing on the goal of becoming an attorney. But what kind of lawyer would I become? What would I actually do with a law degree? Because of my athletic background, I knew that whatever I did for a living, I had to be passionate about it. At that point in my life, there were few things about which I was passionate outside of football, and sports generally. Thus, by the conclusion of my first year of law school, I set my sights on becoming a sports lawyer.

During my summers as a law student, I was fortunate to intern at a few big law firms. I was a bit naïve and overly ambitious in my youth, to say the very least. I remember writing a memo to a partner as a summer associate suggesting that this one hundred-year-old, highly successful law firm, which, of course, had an established growth and business development committee, start a sports practice. I am not really sure if the partner actually read past the "Re:" line of the memo. Nevertheless, when I followed up with him about it, he politely and graciously smiled and admonished me to first work on securing an actual job with the firm before attempting to build a new practice area. Needless to say, that was some pretty good advice, and I followed it to the "T." I began my legal career at that firm immediately upon graduating from law school. I was fortuitously placed in the compensation and benefits practice group where I honed my skills as a negotiator of complex cash and equity-based, executive compensation agreements. During my first three years as an executive compensation attorney, I was determined to become the "go-to" guy in the firm on all things related to executive compensation (e.g., tax law, securities law, ERISA, etc.). Before long, not only did the partners in the compensation and benefits practice target me for virtually all executive compensation matters, but also partners in the corporate practice group sought me out. As a young lawyer in a big firm, it is essential that one stay busy and in demand vis-à-vis the partners for whom the associate is primarily working. Fortunately, I was able to do just that. All was seemingly going very well in my young legal career.

However, with each passing year, I was finding it more difficult to suppress my passion to be involved with professional sports. By my fourth year at the firm, I broached firm management with the very idea I had suggested as a summer intern. By now, however, I was respected as a mid-level associate attorney, and thus had a bit more credibility. My pitch to management was simple and succinct: professional athletes are no different from our high net worth, executive clients and they require the same caliber of representation that traditional executives historically have received. Thus, I would like to apply my skill set as a compensation attorney to a broader client base—one that includes professional athletes. With some reticence, the firm allowed me to dedicate 400 of my 2,000 annual, hourly billable requirements to building an athlete representation sports practice. In that first year, we signed nine prospective NFL clients. Today, some eleven years later, I represent roughly forty NFL clients, including some of the most celebrated players like Maurice Jones-Drew (Oakland Raiders), Matt Forte (Chicago Bears), Antoine Bethea (San Francisco 49ers), as well as 2014 Kansas City Chiefs first round draft selection, Dee Ford. I also represent the current International Boxing Federation Junior Middleweight Champion, Lamont Peterson, and his brother, also a top-ranked contender, Anthony Peterson.

Whom We Represent

From a broader perspective, we at The Sports Entertainment Group at Kelley Drye represent athletes, coaches, front-office executives, broadcasters, networks, arena and event owners, sponsors, content owners, distributors, and other industry participants involved in all levels of the business of sports. When I consider the phrase "sports law," I think of it as including a broad spectrum of services, including compensation matters, employee benefits law, labor law, intellectual property law, trust and estates law, charitable trust law, tax law, corporate law, real estate matters, and litigation. As such, we routinely advise our *professional athlete* clients on a wide variety of matters, including:

- Athlete team contract negotiations
- Athlete endorsement agreements
- Intellectual property protection
- Real estate matters
- Charitable trust planning
- Tax and wealth preservation planning
- Litigation
- Corporate matters

We also counsel our *corporate* sports clients with regard to:

- Creating, launching, and investing in cable networks
- Acquisition and licensing of online and mobile content and technology assets
- New media and multi-platform distribution agreements
- Merger and acquisition (M&A) transactions and financings
- Television programming agreements
- Sponsorship and marketing arrangements

Athlete Representation

To adequately and comprehensively represent professional athletes, each of the above-referenced areas must be covered. At some point in an athlete's career, he or she will undoubtedly be confronted with a legal and/or business matter pertaining to one, if not all, of these issues. Although not prominent in the space, there is very little debate that traditional business law firms are best suited to ensure professional athletes the greatest protection. Because of this reality, traditional sports agencies are routinely retaining general business law firms to provide the additional legal support that is required to ensure an athlete's success (e.g., Creative Arts Agency is reported to have Winston & Strawn on retainer). My firm is the quintessential one-stop shop provider as it relates to servicing our professional athlete clients. Since much of the legal/business planning for high net worth, individual clients, athletes included, is interrelated, it is hugely beneficial to our clients to have, for instance, their sports agent and trusts and estates attorney under the same roof, so to speak. As a traditional business law firm that utilizes a comprehensive approach to advising our athlete clients, my firm easily distinguishes itself from the singularly focused sports agency that represents athletes solely in connection with team contract negotiations, while referring other legal work to outside lawyers and/or firms. The need for the services of business law firms is a relatively recent phenomenon as it was only during the past twenty-five years that professional athletes started earning salaries and other sports-related income that rivaled that of the typical high net worth individual clients that large law firms have historically represented. Moreover, as athletes began to earn more money, they were faced with ever more complex legal and business concerns. Thus, the evolution of the professional athlete to the corporate executive was too prevalent to ignore.

Rewards and Challenges

The job of the sports attorney is extremely demanding, to say the very least. Sports lawyers wear multiple hats every day and all day. That said, however, the rewards of this law practice are plentiful. My greatest pleasure in working in this space is being a part of helping a young man truly to mature into a savvy, successful business executive and to assist him in transforming the financial makeup of his family for generations to come. Frankly, for me, it does not get more rewarding than that. Even your worst day is a good day when you are passionate about what you do and that is very much the case in this instance. It would be a bit disingenuous if I failed to acknowledge that attending every Super Bowl for the past decade, Pro Bowls in Hawaii, and championship boxing matches in Vegas are pretty cool perks, too.

Like any profession, frustrations exist. The same is true in the field of sports law. Chief among the many frustrations, and I would imagine that the same is true for all attorneys, is when a client refuses or fails to heed your counsel. While sudden wealth is an awesome occurrence, for most professional athletes, sudden wealth presents a whole host of sudden problems for the athlete and his or her family. As mentioned above, today's professional athlete's earning ability is very much akin to that of a seasoned corporate executive, lest the latter's business experience and savvy. To illustrate, most executive-level employees spend several years ascending the proverbial corporate ladder before attaining chief executive-level status and pay. During this rise, the budding executive is becoming expert in his or her respective industry and naturally maturing both professionally and personally. By the time he or she reaches that last rung of the corporate ladder, the newly minted senior executive is fully aware of what generally is required for him or her to sustain. The professional athlete, on the other hand, oftentimes begins his career, at least financially, at a level parallel to many traditional corporate executives. At the age of twenty-one or twenty-two, however, the athlete in no way shares the business sophistication and personal maturity of his traditional executive counterpart. While their bank accounts may be parallel, very little else is. Accordingly, without competent and comprehensive legal and business advisors, an athlete's success will undoubtedly be short-lived. Sometimes, this reality is difficult to convey to a twenty-two-year-old multimillionaire!

Additionally, I oftentimes am forced to remind my clients and their families to simply lean on their counsel. The costs at this level simply are too great for the client or his or her family to try to "figure it out." If your plumbing or electrical system fails, you call a plumber or an electrician. It is not wise to attempt to fix it yourself because you read a couple of paragraphs from a plumbing repair book while in line at Home Depot or because you routinely replace your light bulbs. The best practice is always to retain an expert and let them do their job. Watching ESPN regularly will not make one a skilled sports attorney. This point is sometimes lost on clients and their family members. And the lesson learned for forgetting or disregarding this fact is oftentimes very expensive. Such occurrences are most frustrating because it is like watching a train wreck from the very time the train is first set in motion to the collision. Although the conductor may not appreciate what is ahead, you know full well what the outcome will be. Yet, you are not allowed to prevent it. I routinely admonish our clients that if they simply allow us to do our jobs as their advisors, the goal of financial security, and inter-wealth generation and preservation most often will be achieved.

Typical Pitfalls

As noted above, the typical pitfalls occur when a client fails to listen to our advice. The three most common pitfalls that lead to the failure of professional athletes are bad business transactions, marrying without having in place the proper premarital asset protection strategies, and the IRS.

One of the pitfalls with young athletes and those with newly found wealth is that they are anxious to grow their wealth, so they want to immediately start investing money in business opportunities. The first thing we often need to do is remind them that they are already rich and they do not need to be in search of a get-rich-quick situation. The chief focus should be wealth preservation. Athletes oftentimes mistakenly believe that their prowess in the world of professional sports automatically ensures that they will be equally successful in any and all that they do—including in the world of business. On base level, the reasoning is sound. The athlete likely has been pursuing and attaining athletic goals since a very young age. They have typically been ultra-successful throughout their athletic careers—very rarely, if ever, experiencing individual failure. Succeeding has become the norm—a natural expectation. They have grown accustom to winning, and now they are winning at the highest level. So why should they expect anything else, regardless of the endeavor? So, soon after they secure their millions from the field, court, or ring, they try their hand in an arena completely foreign to them. And, needless to say, the result is usually failure. News flash: Just because one is an All-Pro, Hall of Fame quarterback with millions does not mean he can transform overnight into a successful real estate mogul. While we encourage and, in fact, educate our clients on becoming more business savvy, we also routinely remind them that it took them years of hard work, dedication, and sacrifice to become elite-level athletes. The same is true for success stories in other industries. We work hard to assist our athlete clients in exploring ways in which they can grow their wealth. However, we also point out to them that one does not fall out of bed and become the CEO of a multimillion-dollar business.

It never ceases to amaze me how more physically attractive my athlete clients become to certain others as they become more wealthy. I often say to prospective NFL players before the NFL draft that "you're a handsome guy now, you'll turn into Denzel Washington after you're drafted!" The vast majority of professional athlete marriages fail. It is an unfortunate reality, but it is reality. For an athlete to marry without taking certain asset protection precautions, such as requiring a prenuptial agreement, can prove to be financial suicide for the athlete. State laws, of course, differ in this area, but the idea of giving a former spouse 50 percent of your assets after a two-year marriage will quickly secure the athlete client's attention on this matter.

Given the amount of money professional athletes make today, it is not surprising to learn that many of them fall victim to poor tax planning. The audit rate among professional athletes is alarmingly high when compared to that of the national average. For instance, it is estimated that NFL players are audited at a rate of roughly 20 percent annually. The national average hovers around 3 percent. State and local tax counsel is critical to ensuring the athlete avoids IRS pitfalls. In sports, we euphemistically refer to the state and local taxation of professional athletes as the "jock tax." Each time an athlete performs in a particular state, his or her pay related to that performance (i.e., his "game check") is subject to taxation by the city and state in which the athletic performance takes place. For instance, the Baltimore Ravens player who resides in Maryland will pay federal taxes and Maryland state taxes as is required of all Maryland residents. When he travels to Philadelphia to play the Eagles in week one of the NFL season, there will not be much "brotherly love" offered on the field or toward his wallet as the city of Philadelphia and the state of Pennsylvania will tax the player as if he were a resident of Philadelphia. This is true for every state with an NFL team, except Florida, Texas, and Tennessee. Lastly, when forming charities, athletes must become more sensitive to the high-level IRS scrutiny that celebrity foundations undergo. Oftentimes, professional athletes do more harm to themselves than the good their charities provide due to little-to-no charitable tax planning. As for the goal of securing inter-generational wealth for the athlete's family, such is unattainable without sound trusts and estates tax counsel. Probably more so than most, professional athletes loathe conversations regarding their mortality. This makes estate planning for athletes that much more challenging but, as advisors, we must push this conversation—and we do early in the athlete's career. Section 409A of the Internal Revenue Code addressing deferred compensation arrangements is an area of tax law that hugely impacts professional athletes as their player contracts are oftentimes drafted in ways that trigger the deferred compensation section of the Code. As one can imagine, the pitfalls surrounding tax matters are abound and require constant analysis. Without such, the professional athlete client will remain at risk of financial loss.

The Evolution of Sports Law

Player Representation Needs and Requirements

Representation of professional athletes is without question different now than it was twenty years ago. The answer to how it is different is simple: the money is much greater today than it was a couple of decades ago. The NFL generates roughly $15 billion each year and roughly half of that revenue goes to player salaries and benefits. Long gone are the days of the 1980s and early 1990s where NFL players would be forced to work part-time jobs in the off-season, not for any particular experience, but because they needed the money. With the exception of one or two players on each team, NFL salaries simply were not that lucrative twenty to twenty-five years ago. In 1993, the NFL adopted the first collective bargaining agreement between the players and owners. In doing so, it brought two things that changed the landscape of the NFL to the benefit of all involved with the sport:

1. It gave us labor peace that resulted in television networks having greater confidence investing in this product that was quickly and steadily gaining in popularity.
2. It gave us free agency allowing the players to test the value of their services in a free-market setting, which ultimately drove the price of those services up.

Just to clarify, there was no free agency in the NFL prior to 1993; you played for one team for as long as that owner wanted you to play and at a value the owner deemed fair. The NFL was popular, but it was not the golden goose it is today. Today, the NFL's media partners are "doubling-down" on their investments with the league. Previously this came with a considerable risk as each year there existed a legitimate possibility of a work stoppage. The players won the battle for more economic parity between them and the owners in 1993. Now, after three years, NFL players become "free agents" and thus are able to go on to the open market and have teams compete for their services. Since 1993, we have witnessed two significant developments:

1. Television networks began to increase their investments and make significantly bigger commitments to the league. The television deals are now multibillion-dollar deals whether it is ESPN, NBC or FOX. They are making multibillion-dollar commitments.
2. NFL player salaries have risen at a phenomenal pace.

Unfortunately, the failure rate of NFL players since this time has also risen, despite the increase in player salaries. Although NFL players are earning considerably more money since 1993, financial security upon retirement is only being achieved by a vast minority of players. I maintain that the primary reason for this is that the business of athlete representation has not kept pace with the financial growth of the NFL, and thus players' earning capacity. In other words, the services that players needed in the 1980s and early 1990s are vastly different from the legal and business services they need today. It was not economically feasible for big law firms like mine to be involved in athlete representation in the 1980s or early 1990s as NFL player wealth was not at a level that required complex legal planning. The landscape today is vastly different. Athletes are making considerably more money and thus have considerably more problems. Services of the traditional sports agent or agency have not changed during this massive growth period. Thus, what we see today, for the most part, are athletes represented by agents who are providing them the same quality of representation that was being provided to athletes twenty-five years ago.

As for the other ancillary, but significant legal issues—e.g., tax law, trust and estate, general business, litigation, IP protection, and charitable trust planning—the athlete him/herself is left to "figure it out" on his/her own. Sure; good luck with that! So, when it is put in its perspective, it is not at all surprising that the more wealth today's professional athletes are able to acquire, the worse off they are becoming. The fix is comprehensive legal and business protection—that simple. Without it, professional athletes are doomed to failure.

Requirements for Agents and Legal Representation

With respect to the evolution of agents and legal representation, most professional league player unions require individuals to be certified with the respective league's player union before being permitted to represent that league's players. The certification process differs depending upon the league. For instance, the National Football League Players Association (NFLPA) requires prospective agents to have a post-graduate degree and to take an examination covering the NFL's collective bargaining agreement before becoming "certified." Conversely, the National Basketball Players Association (NBPA) simply requires a certification fee and the attendance of an annual meeting. To be sure, the NFLPA's agent requirements are the most extensive of the four major sports leagues.

Once you have successfully complied with the particular league's agent certification requirements, the agent also must be in compliance with each state's laws regarding activity by a sports agent. Most states today have some form of an athlete agent regulation act that defines what can be done and what is prohibited. Several states, including Texas, Florida, and North Carolina, make certain violations of their agent laws a felony event. One of the most notable and recent instances in this regard involves former NFL agent Terry Watson who is now facing roughly ten years in prison for violating North Carolina's law prohibiting the offering of financial inducements to collegiate athletes. He was found to have made financial offerings to collegiate athletes at North Carolina State University.

In addition to various state laws, there are also National Collegiate Athletic Association (NCAA) rules to which agents must adhere. Failure to do so could jeopardize one's license as an athlete agent. In short, the NCAA prohibits agents from offering anything of value to the player, the family or some person of influence connected to the player. A violation of the NCAA rules would likely result in the agent's certification being suspended or revoked, and the agent would most likely be subject to discipline by the state in which the infraction occurred. The agent/attorney also bears the risk of being reprimanded and disciplined by the bar for any such violation, as well as risk of disbarment.

The Life Cycle of a Player and Representation Needs

As the athlete client becomes increasingly more seasoned on the field, he usually becomes more seasoned in life. The client's wealth and family circumstances evolve, and consequently the legal and business services that he requires begin to broaden. It is at this stage in an athlete's career that he begins to work with others in our sports practice. Whether it is the trust and estate lawyer preparing a complex estate plan, the charitable trust lawyer preparing the foundation, or the corporate lawyer advising on business matters, the client has direct access to the expertise required. My role as the agent begins to take a backseat and now I am typically "quarterbacking" it at that point—making sure the client's needs are being addressed by the other attorneys in the practice.

Each player essentially has their own life cycle and our representation of them as a client evolves overtime as well. Our objective is to attract and retain athlete clients who will remain clients of the firm for the next twenty-five to thirty years. They start as professional athlete clients but, with our help, evolve into traditional business clients. In order to achieve that end, we work to ensure that they mature as business people. We first need to help them understand how to utilize the services of the firm. We also work to ensure they fully appreciate the type of protection that we afford them. As they become more savvy business people, they are able to recognize and understand the business opportunities that are presented to them. We, of course, assist them in evaluating and exploring those opportunities and to take advantage of them when it makes sense to do so.

Player Contracts and Agreements

Best Practices for Contract Negotiations

When negotiating player contracts and agreements for NFL players, the philosophical objective is to ensure that the compensation is commensurate to the value the player brings to the team. Once we ensure the overall dollar amount, the focus shifts to the structure of the deal, cash-flow elements (front-loading the contract is most often preferred), and of course, guarantees. Unlike the NBA, MLB, and NHL, NFL player contract guarantees are not "black and white." NFL guarantees have caveats, so it is essential to ensure that the terms of the guarantee are clear. This is a critical point in NFL contracts as they are unilaterally written in favor of the teams. At any point during the term of the deal, a team can release a player and only be obligated to pay the player the guaranteed portion of the contract. Such is a routine occurrence in the NFL, yet players are the ones frequently admonished to "honor the contract." NFL teams very rarely "honor" the entirety of a player's contract. As soon as a team determines that a player's contribution to the team is no longer needed, that team will terminate the player despite there being years remaining on the contract. Front-loading the cash flow of an NFL contract can amount to a de facto guarantee in that so much of the compensation is paid in the early years, teams often become vested in the player for the long term. Back-loaded deals can result in a player being released in the latter years if the salaries are deemed to be prohibitive vis-à-vis the player's contributions to the team. Another component of the deal is incentive-based or performance-based pay. Because this compensation is contingent on player performance and most often other criteria outside of the player's control, it is advisable to put as little cash in this bucket as possible. Negotiations may dictate a performance-based incentive to ensure you maximize total contract value, but achieving the desired maximum value by way of an incentive is generally the least desirable strategy. Salary forfeiture provisions (claw-backs) are routine provisions found in professional athlete contracts. This language most often connected to guarantee dollars are triggered if a player violates a morals clause. These provisions are similar to that found in typical corporate executive employment agreements. Be sure to push back on language requiring forfeiture in the event of an "*arrest*" or being "*charged with*" a crime. Propose that the language be changed to forfeiture in the event of a "*felony conviction.*" As the saying goes, "stuff happens!" And this is especially true for celebrity clients. It is very difficult to remove morals clauses altogether, but if the other side is insisting on including it in the deal, make sure you get the most forgiving language for the clients. Also, be sure that your client is fully aware and understands the consequences of breaching the morals clause. To sum it up, our best practices are to first determine the player's value to the team, maximize the total guaranteed dollars, front-load the cash flow as much as possible, and minimize salary claw-back and forfeiture language.

Laws Regarding Performance Enhancing Drugs and Substance Abuse

As discussed above, the morals clause speaks to the forfeiture of guaranteed dollars. In most professional sports player contracts, such forfeitures are tied to the violations of the policy on substance abuse and performance enhancing substances. A player can put much, if not all, of his or her guaranteed dollars in jeopardy by violating the league's policies on illegal substances. In the NFL, there is a "street drug" policy for drugs like marijuana, and then a policy for performance enhancing drugs or PEDs. When it comes to marijuana, remember that state laws do not matter here. So, Denver notwithstanding, remember that the sports league's rules of conduct trump everything else, first and foremost. As for PEDs, the best advice to players is for them to know exactly what they are putting into their body. It is their responsibility and theirs alone. Most recently, in Indianapolis, Robert Mathis took a fertility drug to increase the probability of conceiving a child with his wife. The drug was prescribed by a renowned fertility doctor, but it was on the NFL's banned substance list. Mathis never checked with the NFLPA and now he faces a four-game (including pay) suspension during the 2014 season. It is important for the player to never trust the ingredients label, and always submit the product to the particular league for verification that the substance is permitted by that particular professional sports league.

Conclusion

Potential Future Changes

Over the next several years, I anticipate that more traditional business law firms will enter the field of athlete representation. As mentioned repeatedly above, law firms truly are best positioned to service this client base. The continued growth of the NFL, NBA, MLB, and NHL will result in a much larger prospective client pool, which currently is woefully underserved and underrepresented. Moreover, as professional athletes better appreciate the business and legal complexities that the current professional sports landscape entails, they will come to expect and demand more comprehensive legal and business representation. Long gone are the days of the singular-focused sports agency. It is a business construct that has outlived its effectiveness. The American Bar Association recognizes this shift as this past year it convened a seminar on the topic of law firms and athlete representation. It is high time for business law firms to fill this ever-growing void!

Advice for Colleagues

The vast majority of sports agents are lawyers, yet the vast majority do not operate in a traditional business law firm. Therefore, they generally do not have the resource capability to best service the professional athlete client. In the end, there is no escaping the reality that to adequately represent you must recognize that today's professional athlete requires comprehensive legal protection and you cannot expect a young player coming in at twenty-one years old to understand that. There is going to be complex tax law, wealth preservation, and trust and estate issues that will require a certain level of expertise. They will not know these issues unless that lawyer or agent affiliates with a law firm and prevents the client from being exposed.

Key Takeaways

- Help young professional athletes understand that their chief focus of their newly found wealth should be preservation. Be sure they meet with financial experts to ensure financial stability and security. As they mature, consideration for other investments and endeavors can be considered with the guidance of legal and business advisors.
- Remember to maximize the total guarantee, frontload the contract, and minimize any claw-back and forfeiture provisions when negotiating team contracts on behalf of your athlete clients.
- The predominate form of athlete representation remains the singular sports agency model, despite the reality that such has failed most of its clients. In today's world, athlete advisors/agents should be positioned in a manner that allows them to provide comprehensive professional services to assist with the multitude of legal issues their clients will undoubtedly face. Not doing so will ensure that the athlete client's dream of financial security will not be attained.

Adisa P. Bakari is a partner in the Washington, DC office of Kelley Drye & Warren LLP and chair of The Sports Entertainment Group. Mr. Bakari counsels professional athletes with respect to the negotiation of player and marketing contracts, in addition to various other aspects of their athletic and post-athletic careers. He is certified as an agent by the National Football League Players Association and the National Basketball Players Association.

Effectively Representing Sports Organizations and Universities

Donald Prophete
Shareholder
Littler Mendelson

ASPATORE

Introduction

I am a senior partner with the law firm of Littler Mendelson. The firm is headquartered in San Francisco and has more than sixty locations worldwide, employing roughly 1,100 lawyers. Along with a number of other lawyers at the firm, I represent sports franchises in baseball, hockey, basketball, and football, as well as the National Collegiate Athletic Association (NCAA). I work on the management/ownership side of these cases, and have been doing this type of work for the past twenty-two years.

Under its broadest definition, sports law involves anything that touches the representation of teams engaged in the sports industry. Typically, the area of sports law is comprised of the following substantive areas: labor, employment, contract, and antitrust. Our firm represents management in issues involving their employees, including the professional athletes who provide services to these sports conglomerates.

Employee Misconduct, Disability, and Discrimination Issues in the Field of Sports Law

One example of how the practice of sports law has evolved in recent times is in the employment law context. Before the advent of Title VII and other employment-related laws, athletes were not necessarily held to the same employment standards as other employees. In fact, it was rare for an athlete to be disciplined for "off-the-field" conduct. However, public sentiment has now shifted to such a point that sports franchises are being forced to apply the same, or similar, code of conducts to its "athlete employees" as they do to their non-athlete employees. The mere fact that the employee is a highly paid entertainer is no longer sufficient to exempt these individuals from the same performance standards as other employees. Failure to properly apply these standards to athlete employees can create liability for their employer.

It should be noted that Title VII—a law that was passed in 1964 and amended in 1991—specifically states that an employer may not discriminate or take improper action against employees based on any covered criteria, which includes *race, color, religion, sex and national origin*.[1] Sexual orientation is

[1] Title VII of the Civil Rights Act of 1964, Pub. L. No. 88-358, 78 Stat. 241, Title VII (as amended 1991).

not specifically covered by Title VII. However, many states have enacted their own supplemental laws that cover discrimination based on sexual orientation. Age-related issues are covered under the Age Discrimination in Employment Act (ADEA)[2], and disability-related issues are covered under the Americans with Disabilities Act (ADA).[3] These laws, and a penumbra of other federal, state, and local laws, create a large body of legislation that protects the employee in the workplace and subjects the employer to significant liability for failing to provide a workplace free of discrimination and harassment.

The fact that most professional athletes are represented by unions, and thereby covered by a collective bargaining agreement, does not exempt employers from enforcement of federal or state employment laws. However, context will matter in the enforcement of certain laws based on the unique circumstances and demands of the employment world. By way of illustration, the ADA proscribes discrimination based on an employee's disability. For instance, an employer could not lawfully discriminate against an employee because that employee has an amputated leg, if the employee can otherwise substantially meet all of the necessary elements of his job. In fact, the ADA would require that the employer provide a person with such a disability a reasonable accommodation to help them perform the essential functions of the job. This accommodation could include, but is not limited to, removing parts of the job that would require the employee to walk around the facility, providing closer parking, providing a special seated arrangement, etc. The accommodation required is based on the individual circumstances of each employee.

However, a similar accommodation would not be required by a professional team for an athlete employee, as that individual's disability would be seen as disqualifying the employee from the essential function of most athletes, which is to be able to move and run without impediment. In fact, in the professional football context, football players may be cut from the team under certain circumstances based on their inability to be the best person for the position. The definition of who is the best person rests entirely within the discretion of the coach and management. Such a similar deferral on who would be the best employee for a non-sports related job would not

---

[2] 29 U.S.C. §§ 621 *et seq.* (West).
[3] 42 U.S.C. § 12101 *et seq.* (West).

exist. To the contrary, the law would require an objective person standard to determine who is best suited for a non-sports job in the non-sports related context.

An interesting case in this area involved Casey Martin, the pro golfer who requested of the Professional Golfers' Association (PGA) tour that he be allowed to use a golf cart during a tournament in order to accommodate his leg-related disability. This is a perfect example of their overlap between pure sports law/dynamics and those related to pure employment law. As noted above, the ADA requires an employer to provide a reasonable accommodation to an employee who can otherwise substantially perform the essential functions of his job. Here the critical questions with which the PGA was faced was whether:

1. Mr. Martin was in fact an employee and subject to the protection of the ADA;
2. If so, whether walking during a tour tournament is an essential function of the golfer's job;
3. Whether he could perform the essential functions of his job with the accommodation of a golf cart; and
4. Whether the provision of a golf cart provided Mr. Martin an unfair competitive advantage over other golfers.

In the instant case, Martin claimed that he would, with the minimal accommodation of a golf cart, be able to fulfill the essential function of the sport and would not gain any real advantage by riding a cart.

Ultimately, the case went to the United States Supreme Court in *PGA Tour, Inc. v. Martin*.[4] The PGA Tour argued that its policy of requiring all golfers to walk between shots constituted an important aspect of the game of golf. The Supreme Court ruled in favor of Martin in a 7-2 decision, reasoning that the PGA Tour should be viewed as a commercial enterprise operating in the entertainment industry for the economic benefit of its members rather than as a private club. It noted that the statutory definition of public accommodation included a "golf course," rejecting the Tour's argument that its competitions are only places of public accommodation in the areas open to spectators.

---

[4] *PGA Tour, Inc. v. Martin*, 532 U.S. 661 (2001).

Antitrust Laws in the Sports Law Context

Antitrust laws also apply in the sports context. Basically, sports teams cannot collude to deprive individual players of certain competitive and economic rights. In reality, every sports league is involved in some form of allowable "collusion" under the nomenclature of "joint employer bargaining." This type of "joint employer bargaining" is allowed under the National Labor Relations Act for employers who are represented by unions in related industries. In addition, Congress has provided an exception to the antitrust laws specifically to baseball, which has never been provided to other sports.

By way of background, businesses that operate across state borders—and therefore participate in interstate commerce—are subject to antitrust legislation. Attempts to control trade and monopolize may be deemed illegal by federal courts under the Sherman and Clayton acts. Baseball has been exempt from these antitrust laws since 1922, when the Supreme Court ruled in its favor in *Federal Baseball Club of Baltimore, Inc. v. National Baseball Clubs.*[5] The Supreme Court determined, although the league scheduled games across state lines, that they were "intrastate" events since the travel from one state to another was "not the essential thing."

At the time of the 1922 ruling, the National and American Leagues were merely umbrella organizations. They arranged the schedules and set the rules, but the business was local in the sense that there was no revenue sharing, no radio or television, and no national sponsors or licensing deals. By virtue of the exemption, coupled with decades of reluctance of various courts to overrule, baseball is the only sport, or business for that matter, that has an exemption to the extent that it does.

The exemption was not considered again by the Supreme Court until 1953 in *Toolson v. New York Yankees, Inc.*[6] George Toolson, a Yankee minor leaguer, sued over the reserve clause (which binds a player to one organization), claiming it blocked his path to the major leagues. In the decision, the Supreme Court did not deny that baseball was not interstate commerce.

[5] *Fed. Baseball Club of Baltimore v. Nat'l League of Prof'l Base Ball Clubs*, 259 U.S. 200 (1922).

[6] *Toolson v. New York Yankees, Inc.*, 346 U.S. 356 (1953).

Instead, the court ruled that when the Sherman Act was enacted in 1890, Congress did not intend it to include baseball—that the Sherman Act was more closely directed to the monopolies and trusts of robber barons like John D. Rockefeller and Andrew Carnegie.

Antitrust exemptions for boxing, football, basketball, hockey, and golf have been denied by the courts. In 1972, Curt Flood's case—which also challenged baseball's reserve system—reached the Supreme Court and although it was again acknowledged that baseball's antitrust exemption was "an anomaly," the Court ruled that it is up to Congress to change baseball's antitrust exemption. Bills were introduced before and after *Flood v. Kuhn* (1972), but none ever became a law.[7] In 1998, Congress passed the Curt Flood Act of 1998, which said challenges to league rules that restrict player movement or compensation would be subject to antitrust laws.[8]

In sum, the courts and Congress provided preferential treatment to baseball back in the early 1900s because, at that time, baseball was truly America's pastime. Society was willing to turn a blind eye to the monopoly by the leagues and team owners, under the guise that a system placing limitations on an athlete's ability to transfer from team to team was necessary to retain a competitive balance. Although no other sports have been provided a similar specific exception as baseball, for all intents and purposes, the same benefits provided to baseball apply to other professional sports.

The NCAA's Role in Regulating Amateur Athletics

The NCAA is a non-profit association that regulates collegiate athletics. The NCAA ensures through legislation that all of its member organizations—i.e., universities—are held to the same standards with respect to recruiting, gifting, competition, and anything else that touches upon the opportunities given in collegiate athletics. NCAA bylaws are limited, and member universities abide by those rules on a voluntary basis. The rules are not legally binding and obedience to the rules is strictly voluntary. However, failure to abide by the NCAA rules disqualifies a university from participation in the NCAA sponsored events.

---

[7] *Flood v. Kuhn*, 407 U.S. 258 (1972).

[8] 15 U.S.C. §§ 12 *et seq*. (West).

The National Labor Relations Act (NLRA) very specifically provides that employees have the ability to organize and unionize for the purposes of collective bargaining.[9] One question that has long been posed is whether scholarship student-athletes are actually being paid through stipends, scholarships, etc., to provide entertainment services. If so, are these scholarship student athletes "employees" under the NLRA, who are therefore entitled to organize?

While I disagree with the overall position, there are plausible arguments that what student athletes do is no different from what professional athletes do, and therefore, they should be remunerated under very similar terms and conditions. For instance, professional football players practice for about fifty hours a week. Many student athletes would argue that they spend a similar amount of time weekly on their sport. As the argument goes, a student athlete plays a sport that requires the same physical endeavor that a professional athlete is required to exert. Therefore, universities should not be able to demand that student athletes provide their services free of charge.

Many who support the right of student athletes to receive compensation point to the fact that the universities use student athletes' likeness on TV, trading cards, video games, etc., to great profit. In addition, university sports teams enter into hugely profitable TV contracts in addition to being paid based on their team's appearance in collegiate sports games. Consequently, there is a belief that student athletes should receive some remuneration based on their sports activities.

While no cases have yet touched on this issue of first impression, there is little statutory or factual support favoring the position that they are university employees. To the contrary, the primary purpose of the student athlete is that of student first, and athlete second. The student athlete's primary purpose is that of a scholastic pursuit. They are no different from musical scholarship students or academic scholarship students. The mere fact that their skill attracts more financial revenue for their universities than other non-sports pursuits does not magically transform them into employees of their universities. Such compensation is not based on labor but instead to defray academic costs. That is the reason they are not provided these scholarships in

[9] 29 U.S.C. §§ 151 *et seq.* (West).

cash or as pay. It is also the reason for which the IRS does not tax this benefit to student athletes. Therefore, scholarships and stipends are not wages under any federal law and playing sports for one's university is not work under the traditional definition of labor and employment laws.

It should be noted that on February 16, 2014, the scholarship football student athletes of Northwestern University filed a petition with Region 13 of the NLRB to be represented by the College Athletes Players Association (CAPA). NLRB regional director for Region 13, Peter Sung Ohr, determined that the scholarship football student athletes for Northwestern University are employees who are allowed to form and join a union. Ohr cited the players' time commitment to their sport and the fact that their scholarships were tied directly to their performance on the field as reasons for granting them union rights. As of the time of this chapter, Northwestern filed an appeal to the full NLRB in Washington DC and the issue of whether the Northwestern football student athletes are employees entitled to unionize is still in litigation and will likely not be decided for some time. Nevertheless, Ohr's flawed decision is a potentially game-changing moment for college athletics.

Employment Laws and Notable Decisions Affecting Professional Sports Franchises

All federal and state employment laws apply to individuals who are employees of professional franchises. Whether they are fully enforced, however, is an open question. Certainly, Title VII's gender discrimination provisions are beginning to be robustly applied to the sports workplace. Long gone is the old adage of "let the boys be boys." The mere fact that an employee happens to be a professional athlete is no longer tolerated as a good reason to except them from the general employment workplace code required of others. However, while employment laws have been in place for some time, professional franchises have frequently excepted their athletes from enforcement of those laws. They simply viewed the world of sports performance as being separate and apart from the world of non-sports performance. For instance, the issue of sexuality has always been taboo in the sports world—that is, until recently, as we have seen the passage of more liberal laws that allow for gay marriages, and that prohibit sexual orientation discrimination. Generally, society now has a more open-minded view of homosexuality. Consequently, if someone on a football team is being shunned or mistreated by his teammates because he is gay, we are likely to see a more aggressive enforcement of the laws in this area than would have been the case just five years ago.

For example, a notable, developing case in this area involves Chris Kluwe, a former punter for the Minnesota Vikings. He was released from the team at the end of the 2012 season. In December 2013, he wrote a memo in which he claimed to have been released in part because of his vocal support of gay marriage. It should be noted that sexual orientation is not a protected category under Minnesota's civil rights law. Therefore, it remains to be seen what his actual claims against the team are going to be. Also notable is the fact that Kluwe's on-field performance was declining and could have contributed to his release by the Vikings.

Again, it remains to be seen what issues Kluwe pursues in terms of any lawsuit. As noted, we have recently become much more open-minded and progressive as a society, and therefore, any discriminatory comments that are made in the workplace—whether or not they are made by a National Football League (NFL) executive or player—will be scrutinized more carefully than they were in the past. As noted, it is unclear what types of claims will be made in this case, or whether the law would provide any sort of relief should there be found to be any wrongdoing on the Vikings' part.

A couple of recent cases in this area involved the Cincinnati Bengals and the Oakland Raiders cheerleaders and wage and hour issues with respect to their work time. Typically, on a game day, the Ben-Gal cheerleaders for the Cincinnati Bengals woke up early to get ready and reach the stadium at 8 a.m. for two practices and autograph signing before the game started. After that, it was four straight hours of cheering, dancing, and smiling. The Ben Gals filed suit alleging that their hourly wages are so low that it violates the minimum wage laws. Similarly, the Raiderettes filed a class-action lawsuit against the Oakland Raiders for wage theft, claiming that the Raiders are in violation of California labor laws, which require a minimum wage of $8 per hour—even for part-time workers (all cheerleaders are fully informed it is a part-time gig).

On the Ben-Gals squad, the cheerleaders were paid a total of $855 for their time as a Ben-Gals cheerleader, although they claim spending over 300 hours performing, practicing, and attending events. Minimum wage in Ohio is $7.85, but some of the cheerleaders' pay is alleged to be as low as $2.85 an hour. The Raiderettes are paid a flat fee of $125 a game, which the women say is a nine-hour commitment. That is about $1,250 for a ten-game season, which the lawsuit says breaks down to around $5 an hour if you include the unpaid hours in practices, events, and photo shoots. And they do not get paid until the end of the Raiders' season—in January.

Similar payment for cheerleaders is common across the NFL. If the numbers alleged by the plaintiffs are correct, NFL cheerleader wages are at something close to or less than those of unskilled minimum wage workers. But advocates say cheerleading is a profession that demands specific skills and not everyone can land the job. It is considered a sport in and of itself and requires significant training that is intensively competitive and physically demanding. It is also one of the most injury prone activities in which a high school or college athlete can participate. A famous squad like the Dallas Cowboys Cheerleaders can still rake in about $1 million per season for their franchise.

The courts' decisions in the above litigation could have meaningful ramifications and implications for other teams who may have a similar payment structure, or do the same kinds of things when hiring cheerleaders Currently, these litigations are in the very initial stages. We will have to wait and see whether the Bengals and Raiders organizations failed to properly pay their cheerleaders. The Fair Labor Standards Act (FLSA), which is the statute that governs wages and hours worked, is highly fact-intensive, because it gets down to the nitty-gritty in terms of when work starts and stops; what counts as work; and what kind of work is considered as engaging in activities for the benefit of an employer versus activities for the benefit of the employee.[10] These matters may take years to resolve, but in any case, the result will likely provide a blueprint for other cases.

Guiding Sports Law Clients

When guiding sports law clients, we will typically look at their practices, conduct an analysis of where we think they have risk or exposure, and make suggestions based on that analysis—i.e., "here is what the law says, here is

[10] 29 U.S.C. § 201 (West).

what you are doing, and here is where you could have some risk if you were to be sued or if the Department of Labor (DOL) commences an investigation." At the end of the day, however, it is up to the client to make a decision regarding whether they want to fix things or keep things the same. Again, our job is to analyze the client's current practices and procedures and analyze their risks based on what the current state of the law is at any given time.

It is important to keep in mind that sports organizations are employers—and not only do they employ the players on the field, they also employ people in their front offices, in their marketing department, and in their cafeteria. They have all kinds of employees, and employment law issues apply to sports organizations just as they would to any other employer. For example, there was a case a couple of years ago involving the San Francisco Giants baseball team, which had some interns who were paid either an hourly wage for an eight-hour workday, or a weekly stipend that worked out to be the minimum wage per hour. However, it was determined that these interns were actually working a lot more hours than they were paid for, and therefore, the Giants were required to pay them back wages. A key issue in this case concerned the fact that you can either get academic credit for your work or you can be paid—you cannot receive both credit and wages. Therefore, if a university is not providing interns with academic credit they have to be paid. Of course, there is a difference between an internship and volunteer work.

Actions That Would Constitute a Violation of Sports Law

It should be noted that sports law is comprised of three distinct areas that are merged together: contract law, antitrust law, and employment law. In addition, in the sports world, employment law often traverses into the entertainment law context. For instance, there are frequent disputes between players and management over image use, pay for attendance at certain charitable or for-profit events, and performance and other types of bonuses. These are perfect examples of where entertainment, contract, and employment law almost completely overlap.

Let us consider a recent case involving the Miami Dolphins. We cannot say that the organization has engaged in any inappropriate conduct, because that has not been borne out in court. However, if the head coach of the team—a *de facto* agent of the CEO of the team—knew that some of the team's players were aggressively harassing a player based on his sexual preference, and they were engaged in physical or verbal abuse, improper touching, or ostracizing the player, then that would be considered a violation of employment law by the team itself. This would be based on the legal standard of *respondeat superior*, which stated that an employer might be responsible for the acts of its key agents—in this case, the head coach.

Antitrust violations are generally focused entirely on collusion in the sports law context. Although teams are all part of the same league and the owners comprise a collective bargaining group in relation to the players' union, the owners cannot take market actions to the detriment or benefit of the athletes. For instance, owners cannot get together and say, "Okay, with respect to the Miami Dolphins, the New York Jets, and maybe two other teams, we are only going to pay wide receivers up to $2 million per season this year; and in that way we will ensure that the market stays low and we will all benefit." That would be considered improper collusion and a violation of the antitrust and labor laws. They can take a bargaining position as a single unit on how to create a cap or a standard salary for receivers, but they cannot collude among each other to improperly manipulate the hand of the free market.

Contract Law Violations

Contract law in the sports law realm comes into play in situations where the parties have entered into a contract, and disputes arise over the interpretation of certain terms between the union/athlete and management. If there is a dispute as to how the terms of the collective bargaining agreement should be applied or what they mean, a player would typically file a grievance under the collective bargaining agreement and have an arbitrator make a decision on the contractual provision at issue.

For example, the New York Yankees recently attempted to void A-Rod's contract. They effectively argued his use of performance enhancing drugs (PEDs) violated some of the performance and good conduct provisions of his agreement with the Yankees. As such, the Yankees argued that the violations were so serious that they were entitled to nullify the remaining years of their agreement with A-Rod. That is a contractual dispute that would be referred to an arbitrator under the team's collective bargaining agreement. Under a baseball team's collective bargaining agreement, a standing arbitration committee comprised of three individuals hears all such disputes. Therefore, these cases do not typically go to court—although A-Rod has tried to take this case to court. However, his challenge in court would be limited to the conduct of the league and the conduct of the arbitrators and not to the substance of the contract. The issue of how the contract should be enforced and determined is an issue for the arbitrators because it falls squarely under the collective bargaining agreement terms.

The Rooney Rule

The Rooney Rule requires that if there is an opening for a coaching position, then as part of the due diligence effort to hire the head coach, the team management must interview a racially diverse candidate, among others. However, compliance with this rule is voluntary, and it does not require that any preference be given to the racially diverse candidate—that would be illegal and expose the team to liability. The same situation applies in the private sector; employers are entitled to ask applicants to self-identify in various categories in order to determine whether they are interviewing enough racial minorities in their quest to improve their racial minority hiring statistics. Ultimately, race cannot be the sole factor in any hiring decision, but race can be one of many factors that an employer looks at in hiring an employee.

Simply put, the Rooney Rule stipulates that race is one of many elements that are looked at in ultimately determining whether a team hires a diverse coach, and it helps to ensure that diversity is part of the candidate pool, which is exactly what private employers do. The unfortunate part about the Rooney Rule is that it does not go far enough. The same rule should also apply to front office vacancies where there is a historical dearth of diverse executives.

Common Triggers for Sports Law Investigations

The primary trigger in a workplace investigation is a complaining employee. Most employment laws provide that an employer has a duty to provide a workplace to all of its employees that is free from discrimination and/or harassment. However, typically an employer is not held liable for conduct that it did not know or would not have known about through regular diligence. So, an employer may not simply close its eyes to misconduct and then allege lack of knowledge. Similarly, an employer is typically held to the reasonable employer standard, which requires that the employer act reasonably in appraising itself of conduct in its workplace. The law requires that once the employer is knowledgeable of the conduct, that it act rapidly and effectively to remove the noted discrimination or harassment in its workplace. The complaint need not come from the harassment or the person against which the discrimination occurs. Co-workers or, in this case, teammates may also make a complaint about improper workplace conduct toward others that they have observed.

The Jonathan Martin-Richie Incognito case was unique, in terms of the way it occurred and in the way the Dolphins and the NFL responded to the conduct. It is a rare case where the NFL hires an external investigator to perform an internal investigation based on workplace conduct between two players. Again, this case is a manifestation of the fact that we are becoming more sensitized to workplace conduct, even in the sports context. In the instant case, Martin complained that a teammate—Icognito—who played along him on the offensive line regularly created a discriminatory and hostile work environment by regularly using offensive racial and sexual epithets toward him. Martin claimed that coaches, management, and teammates regularly observed Incognito's conduct and took no action. Martin claims that he handled the situation properly—by making a discrimination complaint and removing himself from the team.

The Dolphins conversely argued that they were not aware of Icognito's conduct or that Martin felt discriminated against until he formally complained to the team. The timing issue is legally significant, because failure to take action of a known hostile work environment would expose the team to immediate liability. Simply stated, an employer cannot remedy a problem it does not know exists. So, if none of the coaches, trainers, or anyone else on the team were aware that there was a problem to remedy then they could not be held liable for whatever occurred. In this case, a trainer and a coach were let go for their participation in some of the conduct—although, as noted, there is some debate regarding whether Martin ever brought his complaint to anybody's attention.

Investigating Harassment/Misconduct Allegations

Supreme Court law requires that investigations of workplace misconduct must be quick and effective. That standard requires that a workplace investigation be conducted within a reasonable amount of time, and effectively—i.e., in such a way as to uncover and remove the hostile conduct. For instance, if someone were to complain today that they were being sexually harassed in the workplace and the investigation took place thirty days later, then the timeframe would not be considered a quick and effective investigation. To the contrary, the investigation may be seen as defective and may expose the employer to liability. Similarly, if management were to investigate a sexual harassment claim within a day but failed to interview the right people or only conducted very superficial interviews, which would not be considered an effective investigation. Such an investigation may be quick, but it is not effective. Both elements are required in order to ensure reliability and minimize liability.

Generally, members of an organization's HR department would investigate allegations of misconduct. However, in cases where the HR department is too close to management or to certain individuals, an employer should consider going outside the organization—i.e., hiring a law firm, a compliance officer, or some other expert who is skilled at investigations.

In order for there to be an obligation by an employer to investigate a particular situation, the employer must have notice of misconduct, and notice can take many forms. For example, a complaint could be made by an individual, a family member, or a co-worker. An observation could be made by a member of management, or an organization might receive an anonymous letter giving notice of certain allegations. Once notice is received, an obligation to research and investigate the issue is created. For instance, in the Kluwe case, the Vikings hired a former chief justice of the Minnesota Supreme Court within a few hours of the posting of an article concerning Kluwe's allegations. Simply put, as soon as the Vikings received notice of the situation they hired external investigators and interviewed a number of critical witnesses. This would be a textbook response from the speed and effectiveness standard.

Any client involved in a harassment investigation should take three basic steps. First, they should intake the complaint by discussing it with the individual making the claim. Second, they should make sure the individual making the claim does not stay in a hostile environment. In other words, if the person who is making the complaint is alleging that her immediate boss is sexually harassing her, then the employer must take immediate action to remove her from that environment until the investigation is concluded. Thirdly, they should create and follow a detailed investigation plan that includes interviews with all legitimate witnesses and review of all relevant documents. Finally, the employer should take effective discipline against the perpetrator to ensure that the conduct ceases immediately.

My role in this process is to advise the client on their legal obligations, and to make sure that they take steps that remove them from liability. Generally, our conversations are focused on making sure that the client follows all federal, state, and local laws with respect to the claim being made.

Implementing an Effective Compliance Program in Universities and Sports Organizations

The most important step to take in order to avoid compliance violations in sports organizations and universities is to put compliance policies in place that address how to handle misconduct, how to enforce internal policies, and how to provide training on those policies. Certain jurisdictions, such as California, require that all employers provide workplace behavior compliance training for their employees. In California, an effective policy requires the hiring of an outside resource to conduct classroom-type training sessions. For instance, the instructor would train on Title VII; provide examples of what would be considered appropriate and inappropriate behavior; provide information on how to make a complaint if an employee is exposed to an improper environment; and discuss what remedies the law provides by way of protection.

Just like any other employer, sports organizations should have written policies in place that directly address what the law is and what expectations the organization must meet, from a legal standpoint, when it is confronted with discrimination allegations. For example, the organization should provide its employees with proper access to make a complaint to a neutral party, and again, it should provide training for its workforce regarding discrimination issues.

In a university setting, it is important for an attorney to sit down with all of the student-athletes and tell them what types of benefits they can and cannot receive, as there are so-called "impermissible benefits" for student athletes. By way of example, one may want to ask if a student athlete owns or leases a car. You do not want to uncover a situation where some outside party/sponsor is providing a student athlete with a car.

University staff should also let the student athletes know that they are expected to comply with both the NCAA and the university's rules, and inform them that if they know of an actual or suspected violation, there are certain resources they can utilize to report those incidents. In addition, individual sports teams within the institution may have their own sets of rules. For example, the freshmen members of the wrestling team may have to go to five hours of tutoring a week during their first year to make sure that they are getting all the help they need to be academically successful.

Our firm has a number of white papers on these issues that we share with clients, but we find that the most effective way to teach compliance strategies is through presentations, because most people do not want to sit down and read through reams of information; they prefer to engage in one-on-one or classroom type conversations on what the law says in this area. The compliance issues we teach are not specific to universities, the NCAA, or to sports teams, because workplace compliance practices apply to all employers in much the same way—aside from such key differences as the benefit issues that apply to student athletes.

Ultimately, staying in compliance with the laws pertaining to workplace conduct is an issue that everybody in management should be aware of and take a role in enforcing. In most cases, an organization's HR department will work with legal experts on the standard requirements in this area, and a compliance-training program is generally promulgated by HR professionals.

Conclusion

Upcoming Developments in Sports Law and Advice for Attorneys

Looking ahead, I expect to see much more aggressive enforcement of employment laws in the sports organization context; more wage and hour lawsuits; and more sex discrimination claims brought against coaches and players. We are also likely to see more governmental organization intrusions into the sports world. For instance, the Occupational Safety and Health Administration (OSHA) recently started an investigation of athletes with respect to potential misconduct in the workplace. Basically, the kind of exclusion that used to pertain to sports teams is going to disappear and sports organizations are going to be treated much like other employers. Certainly, every employee, regardless of who they work for, should have the opportunity to work in an environment where they are not subject to harassment, discrimination, and misconduct—i.e., a workplace where inappropriate conduct is not tolerated.

I would urge all sports agents and attorneys who have day-to-day contact with clients to instill upon them the importance of implementing good workplace behavior rules, and the importance of behaving properly and staying in compliance with all the legal requirements in this area. I would also urge them to explain to their clients the individual liability that may attach to them if they do not do the right thing—from a criminal and civil liability standpoint, as well as a monetary standpoint. Certainly, both student and professional athletes should understand that they could end up in jail for using PEDs.

As an attorney in this practice area, I wish I had understood more about the mentality of the typical athlete at an earlier point in my career. Most athletes view life from a very different perspective than other people. Student athletes have traditionally been viewed as receiving the "white glove treatment" and have been the beneficiaries of a "look the other way" approach. Nevertheless, as mentioned earlier, it is important to keep in mind that, at the end of the day, a sports organization is an employer—their employees just happen to do something that is popular with millions of people and is in the public eye. Owners of sports organizations and their attorneys need to recognize that the day when athletes got a "free pass" is now over. It is therefore incumbent on sports organizations to ensure that they are compliant with the full spectrum of labor and employment laws that apply to them.

Key Takeaways

- Look at your client's practices, conduct an analysis of where you think they have risk or exposure, and make suggestions based on that analysis—i.e., here is what the law says, here is what you are doing, and here is where you could have some risk if you were to be sued or if the Department of Labor commences an investigation.

- Note that Supreme Court law requires that investigations of workplace misconduct must be quick and effective. A workplace investigation should be done within a reasonable amount of time, and it should be done effectively—i.e., in such a way as to uncover all the bases and elements of misconduct.
- Advise a client who is involved in a harassment investigation to immediately intake the complaint by discussing it with the individual who is making the claim. Secondly, make sure that the individual who is making the claim does not stay in a hostile environment. Thirdly, create a detailed investigation plan that includes discussions with everybody who could be a legitimate witness, and review any documents that are necessary to reach an objective conclusion on the claims.
- Inform the client regarding their legal obligations, and make sure that they take steps that remove them from liability. Ensure that the client follows all federal, state, and local laws with respect to the claim being made.
- Help the client put compliance policies in place that address how to handle misconduct, how to enforce their compliance policies, and how to provide training on those policies. Note that the most effective way to teach compliance strategies is through presentation. Most people prefer to engage in one-on-one or classroom type conversations on what the law says in this area.
- Instill upon your clients the importance of implementing good workplace behavior rules, and the importance of behaving properly and staying in compliance with all the legal requirements in this area. Explain to your clients the individual liability that may attach to them if they do not do the right thing—from a criminal and civil liability standpoint, as well as a monetary standpoint.

Donald Prophete, a shareholder at Littler Mendelson, spends a significant amount of his practice advising sports franchises on matters related to employment litigation, collective bargaining, arbitration, and risk avoidance. Mr. Prophete's sports experience includes numerous matters for the National Football League (NFL) and the Major League

Baseball (MLB) teams, the National Association for Stock Car Auto Racing (NASCAR), as well as for a number of individual team and franchise owners and sports-related entities.

Acknowledgment: *I would like to take this opportunity to thank Amber Hodgson, of Littler Mendelson, for the invaluable contributions she has made to this chapter.*

The Wide World of Sports Law: Keeping Up with the Corporate Takeover of Sports

Travis J. Leach

Partner

Ballard Spahr LLP

ASPATORE

Introduction

I am a business and finance partner at Ballard Spahr and one of the co-leaders of its sports industry group. My background is pretty traditional—I started as a corporate securities lawyer representing companies of all sizes in mergers and acquisitions (M&A), securities compliance, corporate governance, and other general corporate work. About mid-way through my career, I had the opportunity to represent Jeff Moorad, who was a minority owner of the Arizona Diamondbacks and served as its president. I represented Jeff in acquisition of a NASCAR team. This was my first transaction in the sports industry. Since then, I have represented clients in a variety of sports transactions, including:

1. Universities in sports-related matters;
2. Professional organizations in naming rights transactions as well as companies looking to secure those rights;
3. Groups in acquiring and selling professional organizations; and
4. Even certain ownership groups in disputes with other members.

The growth of this practice was the result of working hard to secure a positive result for Jeff in my first sports transaction and then working to develop that relationship. Jeff went out of his way to make introductions for me and provide me with general thoughts on the industry.

Phoenix tends to be a magnet for sports and many athletes live here. Phoenix also has every major professional sport, hosts the occasional Super Bowl, hosts the Fiesta Bowl, and has a good amount of sports business in general. I decided about five years ago that a practice focusing on sports law could be successful here, and the firm has developed and nurtured that idea and built up a client list that includes a number of professional teams across the country in all of the major sports. We have represented major professional sports leagues in various matters. We have also represented athletes and coaches on occasion, although that is more of a referral basis. Universities are our newest and fastest growing client base, which we originally represented in general NCAA compliance matters but have also started to help them take a look at how they can assist their athletes, and what programs they can institute to help them look toward the future in the final years of eligibility. I feel this capability is unique to our firm since we attorneys have broad sports industry experience, representing professional athletes, professional sports teams, universities, and owners.

The nice thing about being a large firm is that we have attorneys with many different specialties that can help compliment the sports practice, and it makes it possible to work with these sports-related entities in a number of different ways. I still maintain a significant corporate securities practice that provides consistent work, but a large part of my practice is definitely devoted to sports. I love this—it lets me apply the general corporate experience I have developed into the sports context, which is perfect for an avid sports fan such as myself.

Legal Fields within Sports Law

"Sports law" is extremely broad—it includes all of the legal issues that are involved in typical corporate settings. For instance, much of sports law consists of general contract review and the ability to spot issues and understand the importance of certain provisions. To this end, the ability to negotiate contracts and the terms therein is extremely important. These contracts range from simple vendor contracts and agreements with front-office executives and athletes to more complex agreements for sponsorship and naming rights and transactions involving the removal or addition of individuals from ownership. Additionally, there is a burgeoning field of general corporate governance and compliance that is becoming more important to the sports industry as teams and leagues establish programs and policies to ensure proper conduct of their personnel.

Over the past few years, attention has been particularly focused on compliance with the various labor and employment laws covering harassment, bullying, and the payment of wages. The situation involving players for the Miami Dolphins football club has brought this to light over the past several months, and I foresee this as a common issue in the future where the sports world will begin to catch up with the corporate world. Similarly, universities are also looking to develop general governance procedures, and internal policies that they need to mandate from their athletic department employees and student-athletes.

The sports industry is also beginning to deal with many evolving social issues. For example, NBA veteran Jason Collins recently became the first openly gay athlete to play in one of the four major sports leagues in America. Adam Silver, the newly minted NBA commissioner, recently gave an interview during which he commented that while the sports world is often at the forefront of many social issues, this was one in which he was disappointed that the industry was behind. I do not want to be overly negative toward the sports industry; I agree with Mr. Silver that the industry has often been at the forefront of many sensitive issues. But the public failures in the areas of tolerance and compliance with employment laws demonstrate the need of the industry to pay closer attention to creating solid internal corporate governance structures in order to catch up to their counterparts in the general corporate world. I believe that the sports industry has realized that with the billions of dollars involved they must abide by the same rules as other large corporate entities.

Current Laws Governing Sports Organizations and Their Athletes and Employees

Several state and federal laws govern how employees need to be paid and how employees and employers need to act with one another. For example, Title VII of the Civil Rights Act of 1964 governs discrimination and workplace harassment.[1] Employers need to make sure that their employees understand what they can and cannot do and say to one another. Other laws that range from those governing performance-enhancing drugs (PEDs) to what athletes can wear during a game are generally governed by the collective bargaining agreement (CBA) in each league. For example, a drug policy agreed to in connection with the CBA would dictate when players can be tested, how they can be tested, what their rights are if there is a positive test, and how to challenge and arbitrate that test. The policy would be agreed to pursuant to the CBA—so there is a framework of statutory and regulatory laws that govern employees in every setting and then there is a special set of league-mandated rules that fall on professional athletes through the CBA.

Each league has a players union that has been established, through a statutory framework, as the negotiating body for the players. The players then negotiate a CBA with the league, and then by virtue of the labor rules, anything that comes down through the CBA or any issues that come up with the CBA would be handled through the union. For example, the NFL

[1] 42 U.S.C. § 2000e (West).

recently was involved in litigation regarding former players suing the league for damages resulting from concussions. The players alleged the league's advice in relation to the danger of concussions and management of concussions was inaccurate and misleading. Besides the general denial of the allegations made, the NFL's chief defense to that litigation was that suing them in federal court was an inappropriate venue because all of the claims from the players should be addressed through the process outlines in the CBA. Disputes under CBAs are not typically resolved in federal court—they are usually resolved through use of some form of arbitration or the labor relations board, and this claim from the former players should have gone through arbitration. The NFL and plaintiffs are in the settlement process now, but this is a perfect example of how certain matters are handled through the CBA as opposed to more traditional litigation.

Shifting to amateur sports, the National Collegiate Athletic Association (NCAA) is a governing body with member institutions (colleges and universities). The NCAA has established bylaws that they require their member institutions, student athletes, and employees to follow. The primary bylaw under the NCAA is Bylaw 12 of the NCAA Manual, which governs amateurism and ensures that student-athletes are able to maintain their amateur status. There are many enumerated rules and limitations that student-athletes need to make sure they comply with in order to maintain their amateur status. If the student-athlete fails to comply, the NCAA will issue a penalty to the student athlete and possibly the institution. A recent very public example of a student-athlete and an institution dealing with an amateurism issue was that illustrated by Johnny Manziel, who was under scrutiny for allegedly receiving compensation for providing autographed footballs. If Mr. Manziel did provide his signature in exchange for compensation, the NCAA would have found him in violation of Bylaw 12.5.1, which prohibits student-athletes from receiving compensation for use of their names or likenesses (or permitting such use for commercial purposes). A violation of this bylaw can jeopardize eligibility and the severity of the discipline is determined by the NCAA based upon a review of the particular facts and circumstances of the case. In the Manziel case, the NCAA was unable to prove that Mr. Manziel was compensated or knew that the use of his name and likeness would be used for commercial purposes. Because of this lack of evidence, the NCAA and Texas A&M agreed to a half game suspension for Mr. Manziel. On a similar note, a few years ago a University of Oregon student-athlete accepted a benefit in the form of cash handed to the student-athlete and a $10 meal from an agent. The student-athlete self-reported the incident and received a one-game suspension from the NCAA for accepting an impermissible benefit in violation of Bylaw 12.3.1.2. Under the current framework, the NCAA must monitor these situations constantly, make sure that athletes do not use or permit their likeness to be used, or take extra benefits from boosters, fans, and agents. Universities must also ensure that solid internal programs are put into place so that, apart from NCAA investigation, the athletes understand the bylaws.

The NCAA also monitors recruiting activities by college coaches to ensure that they pay attention to relevant rules, including blackout dates, methods of contact, and how many times recruits are contacted. In addition, compliance departments monitor financial aid for students and how those aid awards are given—this can be a very complicated process.

Finally, the NCAA is also playing a role in the health of student-athletes. As a result of the attention paid to the concussion problem facing athletes, the NCAA required all of its member institutions to establish a plan for managing concussions. Once the plans were adopted, the responsibility on compliance efforts and monitoring the effectiveness of these plans is with the universities.

Legal Issues in the Spotlight for Amateur Sports

Each entity that regulates amateur athletes has its own relevant governance issues that are widely known and debated for various reasons. Very generally, the NCAA governs college athletes, the US and World Anti-Doping Agencies (USADA and WADA) govern testing of Olympic athletes, and the Uniform Athlete Agent Act governs athletes and agents in most state jurisdictions.

WADA monitors compliance with the World Anti-Doping Code, which provides standards for anti-doping regulations. Hundreds of sports organizations and national anti-doping agencies follow the code. USADA is responsible for implementing the World Anti-Doping Code in the United States. Most notably USADA is the anti-doping agency regulating doping for US Olympic athletes.

The NCAA spends a lot of time and effort trying to regulate the relationship between the athletes and agents. It is a highly visible problem that is debated every year at the beginning of football season. The debate over whether or not student-athletes should receive stipends, additional benefits, or some form of compensation is ongoing. There is so much money involved in college sports these days between ticket sales, scholarships, television contracts, and sponsorships that it is inevitable that this debate will continue. Under the current framework, the NCAA must enforce the rules it has in place, which provide for restrictions on benefits to student-athletes. Inevitably, the enforcement of these rules brings much public scrutiny because the ones involved are the most well-known athletes, coaches, and universities. The NCAA and the universities spend a significant amount of time attempting to educate the athletes and universities on what is and is not permitted under the rules so they do not end up in another very public situation like the one they had with Johnny Manziel, described in more detail above.

Shifting to another spotlight issue, there are two types of illegal substance control issues that must be regulated as well. The first involves illegal drugs banned under federal and state statutes such as marijuana (in most jurisdictions), cocaine and other narcotics. Each governing entity has their own substance abuse policy that penalizes athletes for the possession or use of these drugs. Performance enhancing drugs (PEDs) are the second class of substances that are regulated. Each governing entity will have a PED policy, and if an athlete violates the policy by taking a substance on a banned list, they must follow a designated protocol. PED policies are instituted by the leagues to protect the integrity of their game and organization. Each sport has its own policy, and they evolve over time when new PEDs are used and new information about certain substances comes to light. Amateur and Olympic athletes must adhere to the USADA, which has an arbitration process set up for them to appeal if they choose to do so. If the process does not go the way that the athlete wants it to, he can then take that to the Court of Arbitration for Sport or CAS, which is the entity that has been recognized on the world level.

O'Bannon v. NCAA

Ed O'Bannon, a former UCLA basketball player, sued Electronic Arts, the NCAA, and the Collegiate Licensing Company over the use of his likeness.

This lawsuit was consolidated with others filed by former college athletes and has been partially certified as a class action. The plaintiffs are essentially arguing that the NCAA and its licensing partners violated antitrust laws by not compensating them for the use of their names and likenesses. In 2013, it was announced that settlement had been reached with Electronic Arts and the Collegiate Licensing Co., reportedly for $40 million, but the specific terms remain confidential. The outcome of this case could have an enormous impact on the structure of college sports and many of the issues discussed in this chapter. If the NCAA were to lose, a completely new structure for college athletics will emerge.

Intellectual Property Law in Sports

Intellectual property (IP) issues frequently arise in sports law. Monitoring and enforcing clients' trademarks is essentially the same at both the team and the athlete level. Before a trademark is filed, we like to do a clearance search—our IP team will make sure that they feel the trademark is a good one and does not infringe on any others. This is a due diligence process, and once they feel comfortable that it is safe, they will file for that trademark federally. A number of services out there can monitor the trademark to see if anything else pops up that could potentially infringe on it. If something does come up, we will reach out to the infringer and ask them to stop using the mark and take legal action if necessary.

With all the modern databases and search engines available for us to monitor trademarks, the difficulty lies not in finding the potential infringements but determining which are significant enough to cause a problem. Sometimes the mark will be completely out of use, or will be in use but in an entirely separate area of business. Regardless, as the attorney for a client you must bring this to their attention and see what they want to do about it. As soon as your client has notice of an infringing market, they need to take immediate action because failure to do so may result in your client's inability to take action against the infringer in the future.

Common Employee Law Violations and How They Come to Light

Wage and hour violations have been part of a recent trend in cases in general, and have hit hard in the world of sports. Recently, a former Oakland Raiders cheerleader filed a complaint against the Oakland

Raiders for failure to pay her minimum wage under the Fair Labor Standards Act (FLSA).[2] While the cheerleader was paid a fixed amount per game, which met the minimum wage, she was not compensated for the other hours she put into the job, and that resulted in her being paid less than minimum wage. Another issue that affects the sports industry is the misclassification of workers as exempt employees (meaning they are not entitled to overtime), when they do not qualify as an exempt employee. In these cases, the teams may be faced with class action lawsuits for unpaid overtime.

Wage and hour issues also involve the teams' use of interns. The United States Department of Labor has established six criteria that teams need to evaluate in order to determine whether an individual is a true employee or whether he or she is a valid intern—if so, they do not need to be paid. If the intern does not fit the following criteria, the team could be held liable for unpaid wages. Many states have statutes regarding unpaid wages, and the teams could be responsible not only for some base amount of wages, but also treble damages and even potential criminal liability. The six criteria are as follows:

1. The internship must be similar to training that would occur in an educational environment;
2. It is for the better benefit of the intern;
3. The intern does not displace any other workers;
4. The employer cannot derive an immediate advantage (this factor is difficult to meet because the company must be able to prove that they do not derive any revenue from the intern's work);
5. The intern cannot be entitled to a job at the end of the internship; and
6. The intern must clearly understand that he or she is not entitled to wages. Employers often tie their internships to college credit and make sure there is close supervision of the intern to ensure that the internship experience is educational in nature and not revenue driven.

Apart from these wage and hour issues, the ongoing Miami Dolphins case involving Richie Incognito and Jonathan Martin has a chance to alter the landscape of harassment in team sports. Most of us have played sports competitively at some point in our lives and many probably are familiar

---

[2] 29 U.S.C §§ 200 *et seq.* (West).

with that environment. It is unlike any other work environment, and I think it is going to be a challenge to make sure that it does not violate harassment in the workplace laws. I know that other professional organizations are watching how this unfolds very carefully in order to craft their own policies to avoid having this same thing happen to them. Amateur sports organizations are paying attention too—they are going to want to set the environment right at the lower levels as well. Just as with the concussion litigation, these teams are treating their organizations like a typical corporation and are working to establish proper corporate governance standards, and harassment is just another issue that needs to have structure to regulate appropriate behavior.

Just this year, Northwestern University football players voted to unionize and on March 26, 2014, the National Labor Relations Board ruled that the football players were university employees and were entitled to an election that will determine whether they can form a union. Northwestern has voiced its disagreement with this decision and has stated that it will appeal. Nevertheless, this recent success could lead other schools and player groups to follow suit. There are many questions and different opinions at the judicial level as to whether or not amateur athletes who are not being paid are actually employees who can unionize under the National Labor Relations Act (NLRA), and it will be interesting to see how this unfolds.[3] The athletes' position and rationale for voting to unionize is that they have no collective voice and power to advance their cause. While the NCAA claims to be the voice of the athletes, the plaintiffs argue that the NCAA's actions seem to call this into question. It is important to note that although this is an important development, it will not have a direct impact on public universities as they are governed by the applicable state laws in which they operate.

First Amendment Issues

We have also advised clients, typically sports teams, on First Amendment related issues. This includes situations ranging from when fans can put signage up in the stadium to monitoring protests outside of the stadium. Generally, a balance needs to be struck between the right to free speech and the property owner's right to conduct business and keep the premises safe.

---

[3] 29 U.S.C. §§ 151 *et seq.*

Strategies for Representing Clients

We have significant experience in representing clients in corporate and general governance matters. This corporate background, combined with our work with universities, has allowed us to provide effective counsel to universities and teams in compliance and enforcement related matters. We are up to date on the "best practices," so if there is an investigation or an issue that arises, we are well versed in being able to offer advice based on what other institutions are doing and the best way to respond.

Most organizations I work with, whether a public company or an athletic department, have compliance departments that are responsible for addressing increasingly complex issues. The current trend is to place more emphasis and resources into compliance because they realize that the consequences of a violation of the law, or of a league or NCAA bylaw, are significant. The approach is different with each organization. We rarely represent an individual with compliance related matters because typically a compliance matter for an athlete would be related to personal conduct such as not wearing his uniform in a way that the league mandates, or testing positive for a PED. These matters fall on the athlete and often his agent, because of the constant changes in PEDs and new substances found to be illegal. Often, an athlete's agent has procedures in place to help him become aware of new substances that might be on a banned list, but the majority of the time, the education has to be made directly to the athlete. We are able to become more directly involved at the university level. We frequently conduct annual or semi-annual presentations to either the compliance department or the student athletes to remind them of hot button issues and recent examples of enforcement actions.

First Steps in Advising Clients

When a client approaches us because of a league, agency or organization investigation, we engage in a lengthy fact-finding mission. We ask a number of questions, and try not to provide much of a response at first in order to better understand what the alleged violation and problem is. From there, we immediately discuss it with our internal team of advisors, including our internal general counsel, compliance experts. It is critical to perform the due diligence necessary to understand the facts underlying the allegation and the alleged violation or problem to formulate a proper response.

Going back to the Miami Dolphins case, there were allegations of bullying and workplace harassment. The team issued a statement saying that if the allegations were true, they would not be tolerated, but then they took the time to investigate and work with the NFL's investigation team to interview all the relevant parties and come up with a reasoned conclusion as to what happened. From there, they were able to take the actions they felt were appropriate. The overarching theme of teams and universities becoming more corporate in the sense of structuring their internal governing mechanisms, including human resources and employment law, applies directly to this scenario.

Conclusion

Because of the continued growth in revenue in college and professional sports, sports organizations are becoming more structured and run like successful corporations. Historically, teams were small, family-run operations. In today's sports world, athletic departments and professional organizations are bringing in successful business people to maximize revenues and ensure compliance to limit risk. This move toward a more corporate and business environment is a positive development this corporate culture will help to foster compliance. Recent situations, such as what occurred with the Miami Dolphins, are proving why this is necessary. We all understand that the work environment in sports is not like a lot of other businesses, but the same problems will be, and already have been, entering the fold and must be resolved. The nature of the sports culture makes this difficult, but there must be a balance between that sports culture with the law and acceptable activities.

The most important advice I can give to sports attorneys advising their clients in compliance is to educate them on the principles governing the issues at stake. They also need to make sure that they are available to them and can be contacted immediately to help analyze and resolve any adverse action.

Key Takeaways

- Organizations have realized that with the increasing revenues, they must incorporate policies and programs to ensure governance and best practices. This will limit potential exposure in a number of areas, including workplace harassment and wage and hour issues, which have received a lot of attention lately.

- Everyone involved in sports law and business surrounding the NCAA is watching *O'Bannon v. NCAA* and the other cases filed against the NCAA very carefully. The outcomes of these cases are likely to turn the whole college sports model on its head.
- With all the modern databases and search engines available for us to monitor trademarks, the difficulty lies not in finding the potential infringements but determining which are significant enough to cause a problem. Sometimes the mark will be completely out of use, or will be in use but in an entirely separate area of business. Regardless, as the attorney for a client you must bring this to their attention and see what they want to do about it.

Travis J. Leach is a partner at Ballard Spahr LLP and focuses on corporate and securities law. Mr. Leach co-chairs the firm's Sports Industry Practice counseling professional sports organizations, ownership groups, and universities. Mr. Leach was named a Top Lawyer in Arizona for business/corporate law, mergers and acquisitions, and securities/corporate finance in the 2013 edition of Ranking Arizona: The Best of Arizona Business *and a Super Lawyers "Southwest Rising Star," in 2013 and 2014.*

Mr. Leach has served on many sports industry related panels and serves on numerous boards, including, the Veteran Tickets Foundation, Coyotes Charities and the Arizona Governor's Council on Spinal and Head Injuries.

Mr. Leach received a BS from Arizona State University and a JD from the University of Miami School of Law. After law school, Mr. Leach served as a law clerk to the Honorable Earl H. Carroll in US District Court for the District of Arizona.

Responding to Recent Sports Law Trends Through Internal Sensitivity Training Programs

Joseph Z. Fleming

Shareholder

Greenberg Traurig PA

ASPATORE

Introduction

I work for a large international law firm that has a diversity of practices, including an entertainment group, a sports law group, and many other areas (that relate but are not limited to corporate, estate, tax, labor and employment, intellectual property litigation, antitrust, securities, white collar, international, environmental, and real estate law). We are more than a full-service firm, and we offer many opportunities for attorneys who are interested in various areas of the law.

Before I joined this firm, I practiced in smaller firms. I also worked as a solo practitioner, and during that time, I often had to call on other firms and specialists to assist me in my work. A key advantage of working in my present firm is that there are people you can communicate with who will alert you to issues in various areas of the law that you might not have considered.

The practice of sports law is a description of clients, not law. The practice involves a variety of legal situations, entities, and people. We deal with issues in virtually every area of the law. Many people who practice sports law tend to limit their practice to those areas where they have expertise—i.e., negotiating contracts, litigating issues, or protecting intellectual property. However, on any given day, most individuals who are sports law practitioners may encounter new specialties to assist clients; indeed, they can never cover all issues regardless of their knowledge, due to all of the different issues that may arise in this area. A sports law case may involve criminal activity, defamation, labor and employment issues, antitrust issues, and/or intellectual property issues. Therefore, there are many advantages for a sports law attorney who has an understanding of various areas of the law. If you are not part of a large firm, you can generally with a broad base recognize issues and work out arrangements with experts in other firms and put together an effective sports law team in that way.

With respect to my own practice, I obtained a master's degree in labor law from New York University Graduate School of Law, and over time, I expanded my expertise into the field of employment law. My work as a labor and employment lawyer enabled me to handle some sports law cases as well. I represented a National Football League (NFL) team, and I was also involved in the antitrust litigation that involves most sports teams, because they often take advantage of the statutory exemptions from antitrust law (antitrust laws have statutory and case law exemptions for union-management agreements, which may enable restrictions on players' ability to be "free agents," or move to different teams). I expanded my sports law work because I was also able to practice in other legal areas to assist clients (including not only labor and employment other administrative law areas as well). In one of my earliest cases, I was asked to help an NFL football team determine how to convert the rent that it was paying on a stadium into tax payments. Ultimately, I came up with a solution that involved figuring out how much rent the team was paying per game. Basically, I had to figure out how many tickets were sold at the municipal stadium and convert that revenue—with the permission of the local, state, and other governmental entities—from rent into taxes. Because rent is taxable, and taxes are not subject to double taxation, paying local taxes to a municipal stadium was less costly than paying rent and then taxes on the rent.

Over the years, I have handled labor and employment law issues for both the NFL and Major League Baseball teams and other sports organizations. For example, I once handled a case that involved doping disqualification claims and an analysis of whether an athlete's alleged doping and use of medication was due to a disability, or if the athlete was not disabled, and therefore, the medication taken affected the athlete in an improper way—i.e., as a stimulant.

Evolving Issues in Sports Law Cases

Again, there are many issues in sports law cases, including state and local tax law issues, as well as traditional labor and employment law issues that are a subject of concern for any employer. For example, many athletes try to compete even though they have a disability because they love participating in the game; they love the opportunity to make money; and, they are concerned that they would be benched or eliminated if they were known to have a serious medical problem. At the same time, it is important for a sports team owner to avoid engaging in discriminatory activity. For example, athletes may suffer an injury, go to a doctor, and find out that they have some type of medical problem caused by genetic or environmental factors—and therefore, there are certain activities that they should not engage in such as contact or outdoor sports. Alternatively, they may be told that they can play if they take a certain medication. Certain athletes who suffer repeated injuries will be given a rest period, or are taken out of a game. When an athlete is injured on the field and has a bloody wound, it is important to take the proper precautions, so that the athlete and other players will not be exposed to infectious and contagious diseases. Other medical issues relate to broken bones, concussions, and heat strokes suffered during play. Essentially, it is important for team owners to respond properly in these situations.

The Americans with Disabilities Act of 1990 (ADA)[1] has played an important part in some recent sports litigation matters. For example, a golf game may be played on a private course, but if the game is open to the public, the private course may become a "public accommodation" under the ADA. Then it is important to provide accommodations for people in wheelchairs so that they can see the play or have access to stands where business parties are taking place. Basically, when a private club is hosting a public golf event, it may have to redesign its golf course for disability access—a project that may entail installing moving, accessible sidewalks across green areas for disabled spectators.

Generally, the more successful a sport becomes, the more subject it is to regulation. Sports that are less successful tend to be less regulated—i.e., you do not encounter as many regulations concerning venue-related issues or those designed to protect athletes. Societal trends have also had an impact in this area. As recently as two years ago, no one paid much attention to what is said on, or off, the football field, and now it seems that new rules will be put into effect in that area because of the growing focus on anti-discrimination laws. Professional athletes and team officials may face penalties for improper verbal comments that they made or activities they engaged in, both on and off the field.

Self-Regulation and Government Intervention in the Sports World

All sports are self-regulatory to some extent, and they have evolved regulations, or rules of the game, over time. For example, certain coaches who were incredibly gifted were responsible for inventing the game of

[1] Americans with Disabilities Act of 1990, 43 U.S.C. § 12101 (2012).

football. In the early days, you could run off the field and onto the sidelines, and then come back into the game. However, that rule was later eliminated. Similarly, kickoffs used to result in deaths from concussions, until the NFL moved the zone for kickoffs. Stories have been told about attempts to injure key players, such as Jim Thorpe.[2]

The sport of baseball is known for controversies surrounding its infield fly rule, which was the subject of a classic law note by Will Stevens. Stevens was very interested in the rule of law, and he once wrote a *Law Review* article in which he stated that the infield fly rule is not a rule of law or a rule of equity, it is a rule of baseball.[3] He explained that before the adoption and use of the infield fly rule, players would purposely drop an infield fly so they could get a double play. The rule was basically put into play to eliminate the intentional dropping of a ball, so that you could get extra outs.

The government generally intervenes in the sports world's concept of self-regulation when there are issues that go beyond the game and involve other types of activities of great public concern (examples are congressional hearings on baseball drug abuse due to media coverage and recent focus on discrimination in sports). Judges also sometimes feel they are like umpires and an extension of the sports rules.[4] Some jurists feel they can even compare themselves to umpires. Chief Justice Roberts did suggest he thought umpires are impartial. In his book *Men at Work*,[5] author George Will described federal

---

[2] Going back to "the rules of the game," Jim Thorpe was an athlete whose Olympic medal was taken away because, unlike many other players, when he was playing baseball in the minor leagues he did not change his name; and therefore, he was regarded as a professional athlete who was considered ineligible to compete in the Olympics. These days, of course, there are many professional athletes in the Olympics who make incredible amounts of money; and no one is suggesting that they cannot compete in various events. *See* LARS ANDERSON, CARLISLE V. ARMY: JIM THORPE, DWIGHT EISENHOWER, POP WARNER, AND THE FORGOTTEN STORY OF FOOTBALL'S GREATEST BATTLE (2008). Many sports issues repeat themselves (such as targeting star players to knock them out of games). *See also* Joseph Cress, *Carlisle vs. Army: 100 Years Later, Game Remembered for Celebrity Players*, THE SENTINAL, Nov. 8, 2012, http://cumberlink.com/news/local/carlisle-vs-army-years-later-game-remembered-for-celebrity-players/article_76d688fc-2a06-11e2-a994-001a4bcf887a.html (An Army player, Dwight Eisenhower went after Thorpe to injure him. Instead, Eisenhower was injured. When Eisenhower was interviewed later, when President, he said if Thorpe had been out of the game Army could have won.).

[3] *The Common Law Origins of the Infield Fly Rule*, 123 U. PA. L. REV. 1474 (1974).

[4] *See PGA Tour, Inc. v. Martin*, 532 U.S. 661 (2001) (Scalia, J., dissenting).

[5] GEORGE F. WILL, MEN AT WORK: THE CRAFT OF BASEBALL 174 (1990).

judges as being similar to umpires, because umpires are not impartial and generally have total discretion to move the strike zone. I once wrote an article in which I stated that Justice Roberts may have erred since the Supreme Court can move the strike zone in the same way an umpire can; if an umpire wants to have a pitcher control the game the umpire creates a very wide strike zone so that pitches can be thrown all over the place and even knock the batter out of the box.[6] By allowing a wide zone you give the pitcher more power to prevent access for the batter and you get more strikeouts. Conversely, when you narrow the zone, the batter has a better idea of where the zone is and has a better chance to be able to prepare to hit the ball in that zone. Similarly, if the courts do not want a defendant to face, or be exposed to, an environmental or civil rights suit, the Supreme Court may narrow a player's "standing to sue" or participate in order to create a "strike out zone" that denies standing to file such suits.

Back in the 1920s, Justice Holmes found that the sport of baseball was not involved in interstate commerce—a decision that was codified by statute.[7] However, through bargaining and arbitration that has taken place, many of the privileges that organized baseball once held were taken away. For example, organized baseball is now subject, to some extent, to antitrust and labor market rules that relate to restriction on the marketing of teams, and those rules may impact what teams can do with their players in terms of restrictive covenants that are enforceable and exemptions from antitrust law. Rules may be eroded by arbitral and court decisions; one interesting case in this area that went to the Supreme Court involved the restrictions on marketing of baseball caps, which was ultimately struck down.[8] This marketing issue might have survived the Court's analysis, if all of the money that came from that particular restriction had somehow been used for collective bargaining funding, which was not the case. If, for example, organized baseball and a union had a collective bargaining agreement that required baseball cap sales to fund player benefit programs and allowed only one manufacturer to sell the baseball caps, could there have been approval due to the labor exemptions from antitrust laws?

---

[6] Joseph Z. Fleming, *"Just Like Umpires": Why Chief Justice Roberts Correctly Relied on Baseball to Describe The Supreme Court of the United States*, 5 ALB. GOV'T. L. REV. 286 (2012).

[7] *Fed. Baseball Club of Baltimore, Inc. v. Nat'l League of Prof'l Baseball Clubs*, 259 U.S. 200 (1922).

[8] *Am. Needle, Inc. v. NFL*, 560 U.S. 183 (2010).

There is a Supreme Court decision that says that you cannot prohibit women, including pregnant women, from working in certain jobs.[9] However, there was another decision in *Chevron U.S.A., Inc. v. Echazabal*[10] in which the Court ruled that if your presence on the job could pose a danger to others, you should not be working on that job.[11] Translated into the sports world, someone may be a great player in a contact sport such as baseball, hockey, football, or basketball, but if that player has an infectious disease and continues playing, the player could pose a threat to others on the field. The rules that have been established by organized sports are not only aimed at protecting one player, they are aimed at protecting all players. What if only certain individuals in a protected category such as race, or national origin, or religion, had a high propensity to contract a disease? Could that raise new issues regarding employment discrimination due to a protected interest, or a disability?

Typically, the government does not rush to get involved in legal conflicts in the sports world, because most of the rules that apply to organized sports were not imposed by the Occupational Safety and Health Administration (OSHA)—i.e., you do not hear, or read about, many OSHA pronouncements on concussions suffered by professional athletes. There have been Congressional hearings, however, on the use of performance enhancing drugs, including prescription drugs, which are said to give players extra speed on the field. In most cases, organized sports teams tend to handle these issues themselves, because they do not want their best players to be thrown off the field. In fact, players have demanded that their unions should not impose overly strict rules in this area, and unions have to comply with their members' interests. Likewise, team owners do not want to lose their chances at winning because their best players are disqualified.

That being said, the government believes that it should intervene in cases involving the use of performance enhancing drugs by athletes, because those athletes are role models for many young people. They do more than play a game; they sell products and lifestyles. A young person may feel that the only way that someone can achieve success in sports is by bulking up, and if an athlete feels that the only way that they can enhance their athletic

[9] *Int'l Union, v. Johnson Controls, Inc.*, 499 U.S. 187 (1991)
[10] *Chevron U.S.A., Inc. v. Echazabal*, 536 U.S. 73 (2002).
[11] *Id.*.

performance is by taking drugs, they may feel pressured to do so. All too often, when someone first joins a professional sports team they are thrilled by the idea of putting on a uniform, and they feel it is an honor to play for a team—and then the desire to win kicks in. In order to win sponsorship from the companies whose apparel they are wearing, athletes have to achieve—and in some cases, taking performance enhancing drugs is what they do to win games. Again, thousands of young people who would like to fill the shoes of those athletes in the future are influenced by what those athletes do, and their health could be endangered—and that is why Congress gets involved in these cases.

Prohibiting Students from Entering the NFL Draft

There has been some debate in recent times about prohibiting students from entering the NFL draft. An argument could be made that a young person with the right skills could skip college and go right onto the playing field; others have argued that it is important for future athletes to have a college education.

This argument has analogies in other areas. For example, there was a time when many people were learning how to fly in the military; and after they completed their service they would be able to get jobs as pilots in the airline industry. At one time pilots made a lot of money, and therefore, they were reluctant to retire. Some people were concerned that if pilots were not forced to retire at a certain age it would be bad for their health and the public safety. However, others argued that pilots were being forced to retire early so that the airlines could hire new pilots who were trained in the military—and the military could position itself as a training ground for young pilots and thereby successfully recruit more people. Ultimately, the retirement age for pilots was increased. If sports opens up to high school athletes, can that increase the number of players and force early retirement of "older" players? Is there an analogy or reverse analogy here? Would opening up entry to younger athletes have an impact on older athletes?

The Casey Martin Case and Title IX Issues

When the Professional Golfers' Association (PGA) Tour refused to allow Casey Martin to ride the course in a golf cart because of a medical condition, the Tour's decision had a major impact on the sport. There has been some debate about whether golf is a game of endurance or skill. Some might say that an individual might be able to play better if they were not exhausted from walking around an eighteen-hole course. However, the Supreme Court concluded that someone's ability to win at golf was more dependent on their ability to swing a golf club than their ability to walk, and while some have disagreed with this decision, the PGA had to comply with it.[12]

I once wrote a law review article about rowing, which focused on the fact that without the passage of Title IX of the Education Amendments of 1972,[13] which prohibits discrimination based on sex in education programs and activities that receive federal financial assistance, women would have never had an equal opportunity to participate in sports.[14] At the same time, Title IX has been destructive to other college sports, such as men's rowing; universities have been cutting back on funding men's crews because they must now fund women's crews.

Novelist John Irving wrote a letter to *The New York Times* protesting Title IX because he felt that it was destroying the sport of wrestling; again, a men's sport was being phased out at the college level because colleges must now devote more funding to women's sports.[15] Some have argued that this kind of lawmaking is aimed at trying to make everyone equal on the playing field, even if we do not all have athletic abilities—i.e., if you are a really good ballerina the government could force you to dance with weights, or if you are a really good basketball player you might have to carry around a cement block.[16] Essentially, if the government invades the sports world in an effort to make sports more accessible to everyone, those actions will eventually erode the quality of certain sports. While I recognize the issues with Title IX and the funding of sports, I believe the benefits of Title IX outweigh its disadvantages. But if a private college has to bargain with its male football team and costs increase, will that impact female sports and Title IX?

---

[12] *PGA Tour, Inc. v. Martin*, 532 U.S. 661 (2001).
[13] Title IX of the Education Amendments of 1972, 20 U.S.C. §§ 1681-88 (1988).
[14] Joseph Z. Fleming, *Title IX From* The Red Rose Crew *to* Grutter*: The Law and Literature of Sports*, 14 FORDHAM INTELL. PROP. MEDIA & ENT. L.J. 793 (2004).
[15] John Irving, *Wrestling With Title IX*, N.Y. TIMES, Jan. 28. 2003, http://www.nytimes.com/2003/01/28/opinion/wrestling-with-title-ix.html.
[16] *See, e.g.*, KURT VONNEGUT, JR., HARRISON BERGERON, *reprinted in* LAW IN LITERATURE: LEGAL THEMES IN SHORT STORIES 54 (Elizabeth Villiers Gemmette ed., 1992).

New and Important Sports Laws

Issues in the workplace involving civil rights, proper speech, and discrimination, including the use of terms, have been considered unacceptable for many years in the workforce. Title VII of the Civil Rights Act of 1964,[17] as amended, protects individuals against employment discrimination on the bases of race and color, as well as national origin, sex, and religion. However, issues previously primarily in the workplace have now become issues in the world of professional sports. In fact, I have had many cases on behalf of large media and sports entities that were taken to court when one person in a group made a joke, or comment, using a racial term that was considered discriminatory. The client could not argue that everyone in the workplace used that word; if it offended even one person, there was no defense. Certainly, the law is quite clear that you cannot tell jokes about people based on their national origin, religion, or their color that are unwelcome or that create a hostile workplace, and the government has become increasingly involved in this area. Similarly, the kind of language and behavior that was once acceptable in organized sports may now be inappropriate because of changing values and laws.[18]

Up until recently, we did not have laws that regulated behavior in the workplace. Now, however, many of the largest businesses in the country support affirmative action laws to help people in the military and other walks of life to get jobs. Likewise, many businesses are taking steps to eliminate discrimination against bisexuals, gays, and lesbians, and are supporting same-sex marriage. Therefore, it is likely that organized sports teams will take (or have to take) similar actions.

Helping Clients Comply with Key Sports Laws: Education and Sensitivity Training

Most "sports clients" are engaged in the business of sports, and like the owners of any other type of business, they need to understand that they are subject to certain laws, including laws relating to discrimination, as previously noted. Therefore, as a lawyer in this practice area it is

---

[17] Title VII of the Civil Rights Act of 1964 protects individuals against employment discrimination on the bases of race and color, as well as national origin, sex, and religion. Title VII of the Civil Rights Act of 1964, 42 U.S.C. §§ 2000e to 2000e-17 (2012).

[18] *See Oncale v. Sundowner Offshore Servs.*, 523 U.S. 75 (1998).

important to engage my clients in sensitivity training to educate the management of the teams and players as to employment and special protected interests laws.

Clients also need to be aware that they have to post notices of certain government regulations in the workplace; in fact, you can go to the Department of Labor website and print out posters that would apply to your company/organization.[19] It is important to find out what types of laws might regulate your organization, based on the number of people you employ. For instance, if you employ a certain number of people you might have to provide family medical leave. Organizations that employ more than one hundred workers may have to provide a certain amount of advance notice of a layoff. Similarly, if you are a government contractor or supplier and your contract is of a certain amount, you might have to establish an affirmative action program, or satisfy other requirements. In the sports world, if a stadium is located in an airport zone and related to transportation, there may be a law in effect that requires all people working in that area to receive a so-called "living wage," or satisfy other requirements.

In any case, owners of sports teams—like owners of other businesses—need to keep abreast of the laws that might affect their organization, and it is a good idea to conduct training sessions for your people regarding those laws. In addition, employees of sports organizations should be told that if they have any complaints they should bring them to the attention of management. Supreme Court decisions have held that if you educate employees about the law and encourage them to bring their complaints through your organization's internal system but they choose not to use it, they may be barred from raising their complaint in another arena.[20] The Court has ruled an employee who did not use a complaint system could be barred from suing.[21]

In my own practice, I have been trying to develop strategies for my clients to eliminate discrimination issues in the organized sports world. In many cases,

---

[19] *See* FirstStep *Poster Advisor*, U.S. DEP'T. OF LABOR, http://www.dol.gov/elaws/posters.htm (last visited May 2, 2014).

[20] *See* Joseph Z. Fleming, *'Management Rights' Created by the U.S Supreme Court Decisions*, *in* AIRLINE AND RAILROAD LABOR AND EMPLOYMENT LAW: A COMPREHENSIVE ANALYSIS 538 (2014).

[21] *Id.* at 574. (discussion of *Burlington Industries, Inc. v. Ellerth*, 524 U.S. 742 (1998) and *Faragher v. City of Boca Raton*, 524 U.S. 775 (1998)).

people have immediate reactions to someone or make a decision without investigating the reasons for decisions—which, in fact, may be based on prejudice or prior experiences or improper reasons. Such strategies may include counting to ten before saying something or using meditation techniques. It has been found that team members often improve their ability to focus their mind and concentrate, and make better decisions about their actions, if they engage in meditation. Sensitivity training and meditation techniques have been successfully used in medical settings, and they have been used to train troops going into battle. Therefore, such techniques can also be successfully used by individuals in the professional sports realm.

As noted, it is important to assist clients in setting up an internal complaint system—and that means that managers must be willing to give up the right to say "My way or the highway." That attitude may be acceptable if everybody on a team understands that they are welcome in the group, but when you have diverse groups of people playing a sport, problems can arise. Indeed, all of your players may share the same race, the same color, the same national origin, and the same sex, but they may have grown up in different environments or have different personality traits. When people from different backgrounds or with different personalities are thrown together into a workplace, diversity issues may prevent them from appreciating one another. Some people will naturally be more talkative than others; some may approach the way they handle themselves in a different way; some may be more conservative, while others may be more liberal.

Again, implementing a diversity training program and an effective complaint system can help sports law clients to avoid reaching erroneous conclusions and establishing stereotypes that result in discrimination-related litigation. In addition, if you have a good sensitivity training program in place and one of your athletes violates the law, you may not be subject to the imposition of punitive damages. Basically, sports team owners should try to teach their players to be more reflective and welcoming to others—and if you have made such efforts, you will not be penalized for trying to go the extra distance.

Finally, some sports teams are coping with the issue of bullying. Canada, South America, Central America, and Mexico have many rules that relate to bullying in various contexts. In the United States, we do not have any bullying laws at the federal level, but we do have laws that prevent people from being subjected to a hostile workplace environment based on discrimination relating to stereotypes regarding sex, national origin, and color. Again, I believe that promoting and implementing sensitivity training and internal complaint programs can reduce the problems in this area. Hopefully, as more organizations adopt such programs, we are likely to see progress being made in relation to this issue. The University of Virginia Medical School, for example, implemented a program for people working in the field of medicine which involved the concept of meditating—i.e., taking a break and clearing your mind—and using that training in other situations, as opposed to making instant decisions. A survey was conducted involving people from different national origins and cultures, and they agreed that this program could eliminate a lot of hostility in the workplace and would ultimately enable people to work together more effectively because they were learning how to appreciate other cultures and not make snap decisions that would lead to discrimination.

Penalties for Sports Law Violations

In order to be subject to Title VII[22] regulations, an employer must have more than a requisite number of employees, as noted. Also, if a manager or a coach is not employing a certain group of people, the team is considered to be the employer (not the individual manager) engaging in a Title VII violation—and as a result, the entire team suffers. In some cases, if someone was terminated the court may decide that they must be reinstated with back pay.

Indeed, many complicated situations may arise in this area. Let us say that a certain individual is a law firm's CPA and CFO. If the owner of the firm disagrees with that individual regarding a certain tax treatment and decides that they cannot remain in the CFO position—i.e., they are fired, put on leave without pay, or switched to a different position—the CFO may decide to exercise their rights to complain under The Sarbanes-Oxley Act of 2002[23] (SOX). If the court ultimately rules that what the law firm did was not a violation of the law, the CFO may allege that their reputation was ruined and they were terminated as an act of retaliation. There has been some debate regarding whether a court should reinstate someone in such a situation.

---

[22] Title VII of the Civil Rights Act of 1964, 42 U.S.C. §§ 2000e to 2000e-17 (2012).

[23] Sarbanes-Oxley Act of 2002, Pub. L. No. 107-204, 116 Stat. 745.

In the sports arena, a player may be very good on the field but abusive to others. If the abusive player files complaints, management may consider whether they can afford to keep that player on the team, because they are preventing the team from working effectively as a unit. What if the players complain that retaining the abusive player violates their rights? If the coach then decides to terminate or keep the player off the field, they may wind up facing retaliation issues.

In most cases, the sporting industry is allowed to resolve these issues on their own in order to avoid government intervention. Going forward, however, I believe that we are going to see more issues arise from situations where players are not allowed to play in key games. For example, if I were the head of the basketball union and I took a position hostile to management and they deliberately did not play me, then that action could violate my rights under the National Labor Relations Act of 1935[24] (NLRA) because of my union commitment and protected activity.

Consequently, I believe that it is in the best interest of teams to make internal efforts to resolve these issues through the implementation of internal complaint systems and hiring outside sensitivity training experts—rather than waiting until the government decides to look into the situation. I think that the government is smart enough to know that it does not want to get into the business of regulating sports. Similarly, it would be improper to have a rule that owners of sports teams cannot fire someone because they think he or she is not a good player unless they actually put him or her in the game and let him or her lose several times. In that case, perhaps the team cannot be accused of retaliation—although only the owners of larger teams (if anyone) can typically afford to allow an employee to mess up over the course of a year. At the same time, even if a player files a totally bogus retaliation charge, if they are terminated within a week of making that charge they may then file another retaliation claim, which they may be able to win, even though they did not win on the underlying discrimination claim. The courts will typically consider whether there is a connection or causal relationship to the complaint and the date of the action that is allegedly retaliatory. If you are not playing someone, and it turns out that on the day they complained you took them off the field, then even if you are continuing to pay that athlete the government may enjoin you and require

[24] National Labor Relations Act of 1935, 29 U.S.C. §§ 151- 169 (2012).

you to put that person back on the field. It could be argued that athletes have only a limited life on the field, and therefore, every game counts when it comes to expanding their skills.

Ultimately, as noted, I would prefer that my sports law clients implement a training situation that focuses on the use of mindfulness, along with an internal complaint system, so that any problems can be worked out quickly and internally, and management will have a better chance to justify what they did or fix whatever is wrong.

Conclusion

In conclusion, understanding sports law means appreciating all the factual and legal issues. Keeping up with legal and all other developments around you can assist. For example, what new medical laws may open up not only legal issues but legal sanctions as well? Can "wellness programs" under Obamacare[25] assist in training and sensitizing players and teams in programs to minimize hostile workplaces? Raising issues (such as those in the material) may not create solutions but sensitivity. That in turn may lead to solutions.

Key Takeaways

- Note that a sports law case may involve criminal activity, defamation, labor and employment issues, antitrust issues, and/or intellectual property, or other legal issues. Therefore, there are many advantages for a sports law attorney who has an understanding of various areas of the law. If you are not part of a large firm, you can generally work out arrangements with experts in other firms and put together a litigation team in that way.
- Advise sports team owner clients that they are subject to labor, employment, safety, and workplace environmental laws, including laws relating to discrimination. Encourage sports law clients to implement sensitivity training and meditation programs. Also, inform clients that need to be aware that they have to post notices of certain government regulations in the workplace.

[25] Patient Protection and Affordable Care Act, Pub. L. No. 111-148, 124 Stat. 119 (2010).

- Inform sports team owners that they need to keep abreast of the laws that might impact their organization, and they should conduct training sessions for their people regarding those laws. Employees of sports organizations should be told that if they have any complaints they should bring them to the attention of management.
- Implementing a diversity training program and an effective complaint system can help sports law clients to avoid reaching erroneous conclusions and establishing stereotypes that result in discrimination-related litigation. Also, if a client has a good sensitivity training program in place and one of their athletes violates the law, the client may not be subject to the imposition of punitive damages.

Joseph Z. Fleming is a shareholder in the Miami Office of Greenberg Traurig P.A, and immediate past chair of The Florida Bar Entertainment, Arts and Sports Law Section (EASL). He is listed in all issues of the Best Lawyers in America *(and listed in its current edition for Entertainment Law, Sports Law, Labor and Employment Law, Environmental Law, Land Use and Zoning Law, and Water Law) and in all issues of* Chambers USA: America's Leading Lawyers for Business.

Mr. Fleming has received recognition and awards from Progressive Architecture Magazine *for drafting the initial Miami Beach "Art Deco District" historic preservation ordinance; the One Thousand Friends of Florida Award, for Protecting Cross Creek; the Florida Audubon Society for pro bono environmental work involving the Everglades; the Miami Design Preservation League (MDPL) Justice Cardozo Award for representation to preserve the Art Deco District; and, the MDPL Award for representing the artists Jeanne-Claude and Christo in connection with "The Surrounded Islands Project for Biscayne Bay." Mr. Fleming has represented, and does represent, Major League and NFL professional sports teams; international professional and amateur sports organizations; orchestra; artists; entertainers; and others in the entertainment industries, as well as international and US carriers and other employers under the Railway Labor Act and the National Labor Relations Act. He has also served as an arbitrator for the American Arbitration Association and for its International Center for Dispute Resolution. Mr. Fleming is a Member of the American Law Institute and the College of Labor and Employment Lawyers. He has written numerous articles for the ALI-ABA, Practicing Law Institute; the American Bar Association, the Florida Bar, and other State Bar Association programs and journals.*

Mr. Fleming chairs the ALI-ABA Entertainment, Arts and Sports Law program held in Los Angeles and the Airline and Railroad Employment Law Course held in Washington, DC. He is an editorial board member of the ABA Journal of Labor & Employment Law *(2012-2015). Mr. Fleming was management chair of the ABA's International Labor and Employment Law Committee of the Section of Labor and Employment Law (2009-2012). He served as the initial chair of EASL and also the past chair of the Environmental and Land Use Section and the past chair of the Labor and Employment Law Section of the Florida Bar.*

Acknowledgment: *I would like to thank Rachel Paul, associate in Greenberg Traurig PA's Miami office, for her invaluable assistance. Rachel Paul is a graduate of University of Miami School of Law.*

Conducting an Effective Sports Investigation

Alan Goudiss

Partner

Christopher LaVigne

Counsel

Shearman & Sterling LLP

ASPATORE

Introduction

In recent years, a cottage industry of sorts has evolved in the sports law arena: white collar investigations. Given the public's fascination with sports and our twenty-four/sevennews cycle, it is rare for public allegations of wrongdoing in the sports context to go unaddressed or to be handled quietly. Sports organizations now regularly conduct internal investigations into allegations of wrongdoing and publicly release their findings. While the reports are catnip for talking heads, bloggers, and sports junkies, they present a unique set of challenges for the white collar lawyer. Indeed, while no internal investigation is the same and there is no "one size fits all" approach, recent sports investigations highlight a number of difficulties with which counsel must contend.

In this chapter, we highlight some of these challenges and considerations and draw comparisons to internal investigations outside of the sports industry. We conclude with some thoughts on "best practices" for the sports lawyer.

What Makes Sports Investigations Unique?

Internal investigations often begin with retention of outside counsel and are covered by the attorney-client privilege. Typically, a whistleblower allegation, accounting restatement, or government subpoena will spawn such investigations, which then proceed deliberately, with the benefit of time, to uncover the facts and discuss an appropriate path forward. Indeed, clients often want an internal investigation to assess potential exposure and guide decisions as to whether a self-disclosure to government authorities is advisable.

Today's sports investigations, however, typically do not have the luxury of time, or confidentiality. To start with, sports organizations are highly visible. The same can no doubt be said for banks, hedge funds, or other industries for which internal investigations have become commonplace. But although enthusiasts may be loath to admit it, sports also provide *entertainment*. Segments of the public watch them every week, live or in person. When a crisis hits these organizations, followers expect to be told what happened immediately, and the press goes to great lengths to report on what it believes happened.

This public "need to know" drives the decision to conduct an immediate, public investigation, frequently before the facts are fully known or digestible. From a business perspective, there seems to be little choice—the matter is high profile, threatens the integrity and perception of the product, and consumers want to find out the facts. Trying to conduct a confidential investigation heightens the risk of unauthorized leaks, which poses a dilemma. You can either:

1. Conduct a public investigation and potentially chill witness cooperation (as discussed below); or
2. Keep the results confidential and respond to unauthorized leaks on a one-off basis, which oftentimes provides the public with incomplete, inaccurate facts and potentially exposes athletes, teams, and leagues to embarrassment or liability.

In recent years, many sports organizations have chosen the former path—publicly announce an investigation and release the ensuing report. Some noteworthy examples include:

> In October 2013, media reports surfaced that the Miami Dolphins' left tackle Jonathan Martin stormed out of practice after a "prank" went awry. The NFL ordered an investigation in the wake of press reports about these events, including ESPN's release of a transcript of a vulgar voice-mail message (with a racial slur) left for Martin by fellow offensive lineman Richie Incognito.[1] As the Martin Report described: "[i]n the days following Martin's departure from the team, turmoil ensued within the Dolphins organization, and media reports of bullying elicited vocal and mixed reactions from NFL players, analysts and fans."[2] The Dolphins asked NFL Commissioner Roger Goodell to conduct an independent investigation, and Goodell retained a law

[1] THEODORE V. WELLS, JR., ET AL., PAUL, WEISS, RIFKIND, WHARTON & GARRISON LLP, REPORT TO THE NATIONAL FOOTBALL LEAGUE CONCERNING ISSUES OF WORKPLACE CONDUCT AT THE MIAMI DOLPHINS (2014) [hereinafter "Martin Investigation" or "Martin Report"].
[2] *Id.* at 6.

firm to investigate the bullying allegations. Commissioner Goodell announced that "[b]ecause of the extraordinary public interest in this matter. . . the full Report as presented to [Commissioner Goodell], without any redactions or modifications, [would] be released to the public."[3]

On November 4, 2011, the Attorney General of the Commonwealth of Pennsylvania filed multiple criminal charges against former Pennsylvania State University (Penn State) football coach Jerry Sandusky related to the alleged sexual abuse of children.[4] On November 21, after the charges spurred a firestorm of publicity, the Special Investigations Task Force on behalf of Penn State Board of Trustees commissioned an investigation with a public report into the failure of university personnel to respond to, and report on, the alleged sexual abuse.[5]

In 2008, the commissioner of the National Basketball Association (NBA) ordered an investigation into the NBA's officiating program after the Federal Bureau of Investigation and the United States Attorney's Office for the Eastern District of New York notified the league that one of its referees, Tim Donaghy, "had placed bets on NBA games, including games he had officiated" and "disclosed confidential NBA information [to bookies] for use in betting on NBA games."[6] After Donaghy pled guilty to conspiracy to commit wire fraud and conspiracy to transmit wagering information, the NBA announced

---

[3] *Id.* at 54.

[4] LOUIS FREEH, FREEH SPORKIN & SULLIVAN, LLP, REPORT OF THE SPECIAL INVESTIGATIVE COUNSEL REGARDING THE ACTIONS OF THE PENNSYLVANIA STATE UNIVERSITY RELATED TO THE CHILD SEXUAL ABUSE COMMITTEE BY GERALD A. SANDUSKY 13 (2012) [hereinafter "Sandusky Investigation" or "Sandusky Report"].

[5] Press Release, Penn State University, Former FBI director Freeh to conduct independent investigation (November 21, 2011), *available at* http://news.psu.edu/story/153530/2011/11/21/former-fbi-director-freeh-conduct-independent-investigation.

[6] LAWRENCE B. PEDOWITZ, WACHTELL, LIPTON, ROSEN & KATZ, REPORT TO THE BOARD OF GOVERNORS OF THE NATIONAL BASKETBALL ASSOCIATION ES-1 (2008) [hereinafter "Donaghy Investigation" or "Donaghy Report"].

> "a review of the League's officiating program" that would be reported "to the League and the public."[7]
>
> In 2006, the commissioner of Major League Baseball (MLB) ordered an investigation into steroid use by baseball players after the publication of Mark Fainaru-Wada and Lance Williams's book *Game of Shadows*:[8] "a book that contained allegations about the illegal use of performance enhancing substances by major league players that were supplied by [the Bay Area Laboratory Co-operative ("BALCO")] and the personal trainer Greg Anderson."[9] Major League Baseball's initiation of this investigation also "pledged that [the MLB Report], when completed, would be made public."[10]

These recent investigations contrast with sports investigations from just twenty-five years ago, which bore a closer resemblance to classic white collar investigations. John Dowd's investigation into allegations that former MLB player Pete Rose bet on baseball games, for example, was quietly commissioned by the league.[11] Unlike recent investigations, MLB did not announce that the report would be made public at the outset. In fact, Dowd's report was only released as part of a court proceeding *initiated by Rose*, who went to court in an ill-fated attempt to obtain an injunction restraining MLB from formally finding that Rose bet on baseball and would be banned from the game.[12]

As we explain below, the public nature of recent sports investigations poses some unique obstacles for the sports lawyer conducting the investigation.

---

[7] *Id.* at 1-2
[8] MARK FAINARU-WADA & LANCE WILLIAMS, GAME OF SHADOWS (Gotham 2006).
[9] GEORGE J. MITCHELL, DLA PIPER US LLP, REPORT TO THE COMMISSIONER OF BASEBALL OF AN INDEPENDENT INVESTIGATION INTO THE ILLEGAL USE OF STEROIDS AND OTHER PERFORMANCE ENHANCING SUBSTANCES BY PLAYERS IN MAJOR LEAGUE BASEBALL SR-17 (2007) [hereinafter "MLB Investigation" or "MLB Report"].
[10] MLB Report at SR-3.
[11] JOHN M. DOWD, REPORT TO THE COMMISSIONER (1989) [hereinafter "Rose Investigation" or "Rose Report"]
[12] Associated Press, *The Pete Rose Investigation: Rose Bet on Reds, Report Charges: Baseball Investigation Alleges He Set Up a Gambling Network*, L.A. TIMES (June 27, 1989), *available at* http://articles.latimes.com/1989-06-27/sports/sp-4291_1_rose-bet-225-page-report-reds-games.

Handling the Public Sports Investigation

So what are some of these challenges and how should an effective sports lawyer deal with them? Below we outline three key issues for sports lawyers to consider when conducting internal investigations, each of which played a role in a recent investigative report of a sports-related matter.

Investigation Obstacles to Overcome: Encouraging Witness Cooperation and Addressing Requests for Confidentiality

A hurdle all lawyers must clear when conducting an investigation is witness cooperation.

One of the many benefits that the grand jury provides to federal prosecutors is simple: secrecy.[13] The secrecy of grand jury proceedings enables the government to investigate crimes without alerting the targets of investigations, and protects targets from public condemnation prior to the grand jury returning an indictment. The confidentiality of these proceedings goes a long way toward allaying witness concerns about public identification and reprisals for cooperation. While witnesses can never be assured of continued anonymity, they can take comfort knowing that their cooperation with a grand jury investigation may never be publicly disclosed or shared with the target of an investigation. Even interviews of witnesses outside the presence of the grand jury are protected; federal agents do not publicly disclose such statements as a matter of course, and federal statutes do not require the production of prior statements of a testifying witness until after that witness has testified.[14]

While internal investigations are not cloaked with the same legal requirements of secrecy, they often are conducted in the shadows, on a strictly "need to know" basis, even within the business organization. Interviews and reports of internal investigations are typically protected by

[13] *See* FED. R. CRIM. P. 6(e)(2) (providing that various individuals—including sitting grand jurors—"must not disclose a matter occurring before the grand jury").

[14] *See* 18 U.S.C. § 3500 (West) (the Jenks Act). In practice, federal prosecutors often disclose such prior witness statements before the commencement of trial, many times pursuant to court order. Indeed, a key event in federal criminal trials is the date on which such statements are disclosed to the defense. At that point, a defendant learns for certain which witnesses have elected to cooperate against him/her and testify.

the attorney-client or work product privileges, such that they are not discoverable in criminal or civil litigation absent a knowing waiver by the company.[15] And while such reports sometimes are voluntarily disclosed to government authorities, various government privileges can protect such reports from disclosure to the public.

While the advantages of confidentiality are multi-fold, the lawyer conducting an internal investigation for a sports organization often does not enjoy them. Since many sports investigations are commissioned at the outset with the express understanding that results will be publicly disclosed, there is always a risk of chilling witness cooperation. Indeed, many of the assurances that counsel can provide company witnesses in internal investigations—relating to privilege (with the necessary *Upjohn* warnings[16]) and the purpose/goal of investigations—simply do not resonate or cannot be provided in the sports context, where findings will be made public.

While early sports investigations did not have to face this issue—the Rose Investigation, for example, was not meant for public release, identified every witness or source by name, and did not even cite confidentiality concerns—recent reports of sports investigations highlight this problem. The MLB Report, for example, noted that baseball players were terrified of breaching a form of "omerta" that governed players:

> In the course of this investigation, examples of the "code of silence" were abundant. A number of witnesses, for example, claimed that they knew nothing about steroids, never saw

[15] In a recent decision, *see United States ex rel. Barko v. Halliburton Co.*, 1:05-CV-1276, 2014 WL 1016784 (D.D.C. Mar. 6, 2014), a district court found that internal investigation reports were not protected by the attorney-client privilege or the work product privilege because the investigations were part of a "routine corporate, and apparently ongoing, compliance investigation required by regulatory law and corporate policy." *Id.* at *6. In so holding, however, the Court emphasized that the investigations were done in the ordinary course of business, the interview subjects were never told that the investigations were for the purpose of obtaining legal advice and the interviewers were non-attorneys. *Id.* at *6-8.

[16] After the U.S. Supreme Court's decision in *Upjohn Co. v. United States*, 449 U.S. 383 (1981), attorneys conducting internal investigations on behalf of corporations routinely advise employee interview subjects that the attorneys represent the corporation (not the individual), and that the corporation (rather than the employee) holds any privilege that applies to the interview.

> anything involving steroids, and had never even heard the word "steroids" used in a major league clubhouse, not even in connection with such high-profile issues as the leaked BALCO grand jury testimony, the publicity about Barry Bonds, the March 2005 congressional hearings, Rafael Palmeiro's failed drug test thereafter, or the Jason Grimsley search warrant affidavit in June 2006 . . . . one former player told of annual players-only meetings during which teammates reminded one another that any personal information they learned during the season needed to be kept in "the family." He said that players understood that a failure to abide by this unwritten rule would sound the death knell for their careers. Through his lawyer, another former player who admitted his own use of performance enhancing substances claimed that his career as a major league coach would be harmed "perhaps fatally" if he were required to identify other players who had admitted to him that they had used steroids."[17]

Similarly, in the Martin investigation, when counsel uncovered racially tinged abuse of an assistant trainer (who the Martin Report did not identify by name), they noted: "[w]hen interviewed about these matters, the Assistant Trainer initially pleaded that he not be required to answer certain questions, implying that he could not be forthright because he was concerned about losing the trust of the players"[18] and that "he could not be candid with us because he was concerned about losing the trust of the players, which he felt would compromise his ability to perform his job"[19]

It is therefore inevitable that some witnesses will request confidentiality of their interviews, or that their names be withheld or redacted from any public report. Granting such requests should be based on the particular facts of each case. The credibility of the investigative report hinges to a large extent on identifying the basis for certain key witness statements (i.e., what was the witness's relationship with the "target" of the investigation, how often did they speak, how close was the witness to the events at issue?) All such factors are harder to evaluate when the

[17] *See* MLB Report *supra* n. 9 at 88.
[18] *See* Martin Report *supra* n. 1 at 23.
[19] *See* Martin Report *supra* n. 1 at 85.

witness's identity is unknown, and critics will seize on such uncertainty in an effort to discredit the report.

Indeed, the Sandusky Report has been criticized for withholding the names of many witnesses who "spoke with the Special Investigation Counsel."[20] In an extended response to the Sandusky Report, King & Spalding (hired by the family of former Penn State head football coach Joe Paterno) argued that "[w]ithout an understanding of who actually made the statements set forth in the [Sandusky] Report, there is no way for the reader to weigh the credibility or reliability of witnesses or the consistency of statements among witnesses."[21] This is one reason why federal courts have imposed strict limits on parties' efforts to shield public disclosure of the names or appearances of witnesses who testify in open court. While internal investigations and reports are not trials, and there are no corresponding constitutional due process concerns, identifying sources helps the reader assess the credibility of a witness's statement and the investigator's conclusions.

Facts to consider in granting requests for anonymity should include whether a witness's statement is corroborative or the sole piece of evidence on a particular point, whether identification is essential for credibility purposes, and whether there are concerns over witness retaliation. Where possible and necessary, there are benefits to honoring such witness requests for confidentiality. In part, this will promote cooperation with the investigation and potentially encourage more witnesses to come forward. And, given the highly public nature of these investigations and reports, it does protect percipient witnesses—i.e., those who were neither the targets nor subjects of an investigation—from unwanted public scrutiny.

Anticipating this type of criticism, the Martin Report addressed its rationale for protecting the confidentiality of certain witnesses:

> Because of the extraordinary public interest in this matter, the Commissioner made the decision that the full

---

[20] *See* Sandusky Report *supra* n. 4 at 10.

[21] Wick Sollers, et al., *Critique of the Freeh Report: The Rush To Injustice Regarding Joe Paterno*, 10 (2013).

> Report as presented to him, without any redactions or modifications, will be released to the public. Accordingly, we attempted to protect the privacy of certain individuals whom we interviewed or wrote about, recognizing that many of them never asked to be dragged into the spotlight. In some cases, witnesses specifically asked that their identities remain confidential—a few even seemed to fear potential retaliation for cooperating with our inquiry—and we honored their requests.[22]

The Martin Report stated that its decision "to respect the privacy or protect the confidentiality of certain individuals, particularly on very personal and sensitive subjects," did not "in any way compromise[] the integrity of this Report."[23] In part, this no doubt was because the key parties to the investigation—Martin and Incognito—went on the record, and because counsel developed a highly probative documentary record (discussed below), which rendered many of the witnesses' statements corroborative.

The Sandusky Report also cited examples of witness concerns over retaliation, which understandably played a significant factor in lawyers' decision to withhold the witnesses' names. A janitor told investigators, for example, that "reporting the incident 'would have been like going against the President of the United States in my eyes . . . . I know Paterno has so much power, if he wanted to get rid of someone, I would have been gone."[24] The Sandusky Report also added that when documents that suggested criminal activity were found, the investigators "immediately provided these documents to law enforcement."[25] Where there is a parallel criminal investigation and the sports investigator is cooperating with authorities, it is possible that authorities will request that the lawyers conducting the investigation withhold production of names, especially of non-public figures. If such witnesses turn out to be key witnesses in a criminal case, for example, authorities want to ensure they are not placed in harm's way or approached by private parties regarding their expected testimony.

---

[22] *See* Martin Report *supra* n. 1 at 54.
[23] *Id.*
[24] *See* Sandusky Report *supra* n. 4 at 65.
[25] *Id.* at 11.

In addition, certain confidentiality issues contained in collective bargaining agreements between a league and its players may require the withholding of the identities of sources. According to the MLB Report, "[t]he Commissioner retained the right to prohibit publication in this report of any information that he is under a legal duty to keep confidential."[26] The MLB Report also noted that counsel were "not permitted to identify either [one] former player with whom we spoke or [a] current player who [admitted steroid use to the former player who met with investigators] because the Commissioner's Office and the Players Association have concluded that for [investigators] to do so would violate the confidentiality provisions" of the Major League Baseball Joint Drug Prevention and Treatment Program.[27]

Nonetheless, there are practical limits to a sports lawyer's ability to ensure witness confidentiality in public reports. Given the public visibility of athletes, the limited number of members of sports teams, and the press reports covering the allegations that form the basis of an investigation, the public often can figure out the names of key witnesses even if the lawyer refers to them by pseudonym or alias in the report. Even so, in our current information age, much can be said for shielding a witness's name from search engine hits over the Internet.

<u>Obtaining and Executing a Broad Investigative Mandate and Highlighting the Limitations of the Investigation in Any Reports</u>

The public nature of sports reports also heightens the need for the investigation's thoroughness and completeness. This is especially true given the broad scope of these investigations. Drafters of the Sandusky Report, for example, were given almost unlimited authority to "[i]dentify any failures and their causes on the part of individuals associated with the University at any level or in any office, or gaps in administrative processes

---

[26] *See* MLB Report *supra* n. 9 at SR-5.

[27] *Id.* at SR-27.The Major League Baseball Join Drug Prevention and Treatment Program is a collectively bargained agreement for testing players for illegal drugs, including performance enhancing drugs. *See* MAJOR LEAGUE BASEBALL'S JOINT DRUG PREVENTION AND TREATMENT PROGRAM, *available at* http://mlb.mlb.com/pa/pdf/jda.pdf. Under Sections 5 and 6 of the agreement, both MLB and the league are required to keep the identities of players who have failed tests or are in treatment confidential, subject to certain exceptions. *Id.* at 19-20.

that precluded the timely and accurate reporting of, or response to, reports of these incidents."[28] An investigation into Billy Hunter, the director of the NBA Players Association (NBPA), initially probed whether Hunter had violated federal law, but also used its broad mandate to address whether Hunter breached his fiduciary duty to the union, failed to manage conflicts of interest, improperly used union funds, and engaged in nepotism. In opining on these issues, the Hunter Report recounted various alleged misdeeds by Hunter.[29]

Since the sports lawyer typically plays the role of prosecutor, judge, and jury in a highly visible case with broad findings that will be made public, great care must be taken with conclusions and methodology. To be thorough, it is necessary to have the full cooperation of the leagues and teams in conducting the investigation and to make clear that there are no limits or "filtering" of documents that can be reviewed or witnesses whom can be interviewed. The Martin Report, for example, indicated that "[t]here were no constraints placed on our work or that were aimed to guide our results, not from the NFL, the NFLPA, the Dolphins or any player"[30] and that counsel "had authority to request interviews of anyone deemed to have relevant information, including present and former NFL players, coaches, staff and personnel. We were given access to pertinent documents from the NFL and the Dolphins."[31] Similarly, when the Sandusky investigation was announced, the trustee stated: "No one is above scrutiny . . . [investigators have] complete rein to follow any lead, to look into every corner of the University to get to the bottom of what happened and then to make recommendations that ensure that it never happens again."[32] The Sandusky Report noted that it "operated with total independence," "maintained a secure workspace that was separate from all other University offices and classrooms," and "had unfettered access to University staff, as well as to data and documents maintained throughout the University."[33]

---

[28] *See* Sandusky Report *supra* n. 4 at 9.
[29] THEODORE V. WELLS, JR., ET AL, PAUL, WEISS, RIFKIND, WHARTON & GARRISON LLP, REPORT TO THE SPECIAL COMMITTEE OF THE NATIONAL BASKETBALL PLAYERS ASSOCIATION CONCERNING THE LEADERSHIP AND BUSINESS PRACTICES OF THE NBPA 1-2 (2013) [hereinafter "Hunter Investigation" or "Hunter Report"].
[30] *See* Martin Report *supra* n. 1 at 7.
[31] *See* Martin Report *supra* n. 1 at 52.
[32] *See* Sandusky Report *supra* n. 4 at 11.
[33] *Id.*

Nonetheless, there are limits to the completeness of any internal investigation. Even when the leagues and teams proffer complete cooperation, counsel lacks the tools to compel the production of documents from outside parties, or the statements of witnesses. This topic is frequently highlighted in investigative reports:

> "The cooperation of all persons and entities that assisted this investigation—including by providing relevant documents—was voluntary, although Miami Dolphins management encouraged players and personnel to cooperate with the investigation. As the investigation was not part of any official proceeding, we did not have the power to issue subpoenas or otherwise possess the ability to compel witnesses to make statements or produce documents . . . [but] Martin, Incognito, the NFL and the Dolphins organization all provided written materials to us and cooperated fully."[34]
>
> During the Hunter Investigation, Prim Capital, the NBPA's financial advisor, abruptly refused to "comply with requests for documents and information concerning important questions."[35] While such a refusal could be addressed through a motion to compel in a criminal investigation, the NBA did not have such recourse. Instead, "[a]s a result of Prim's refusal to give us highly relevant information, we are not able to provide analysis or findings about the propriety of Prim's relationship with the Union."[36]

Such a turn of events can be unavoidable in internal investigations, which is one reason why the power of the grand jury can never be understated. Where such barriers arise in internal investigations, however, it is essential to document these occurrences in the investigative report, and to identify whether they limit in any way the conclusions that were reached. This is necessary to ensure the credibility and accuracy of the report, and this protection allows the reader to take these limitations into account in weighing/assessing competing inferences from the report's findings.

---

[34] *See* Martin Report *supra* n. 1 at 55.
[35] *See* Hunter Report *supra* n. 29 at 19.
[36] *See* Hunter Report *supra* n. 29 at 19.

Moreover, negative potential outcomes for the investigator include reporting on no findings of wrongdoing, only later to discover from the government or private parties that such evidence existed. Such a result—which can be unavoidable in some instances if witnesses lie or documents are compromised—inevitably arouses suspicions of white-washing or cover-up. Documenting the scope of the investigative plan—such as the individuals who were interviewed, the documents that were reviewed, and the electronic mailboxes that were searched—as well as any limitations placed on that plan, is essential. In short, reporting on the process that led to the ultimate conclusion is just as important as reporting on the conclusion.

Thus, while the MLB Report Investigation famously named baseball players who used steroids, it explained that it limited those names to those whom it found credible evidence of steroid use, and "No player is identified in this report on the basis of mere suspicion or speculation."[37] Specifically, the MLB Report only named players who were identified by two key witnesses, or pursuant to allegations supported by "(a) checks; (b) prior consistent statements; (c) a statement made about a player's use where the witness was a friend of the player identified and under circumstances in which the witness faced criminal exposure for making a false statement; (d) statements reporting a witness's direct observation of the player using a performance-enhancing substance; or (e) the player's own admission of his use."[38] This explanation provided the public with a helpful benchmark in assessing the report's conclusions of steroid use.

Finally, providing the targets of the investigation with an opportunity to respond to public allegations, or to present their side of the story, will help ensure the appearance of impartiality and a complete record. In the MLB Report, "each current or former player about whom allegations were received of the illegal possession or use of performance enhancing substances [was invited to meet with investigators] so that [investigators] could inform [players] of the evidence supporting the allegations and give [each player] a chance to respond. The explanations provided by those players who we did interview were taken into account and are reflected in this report."[39] Indeed,

[37] *See* MLB Report *supra* n. 9 at SR-21.
[38] *See* MLB Report *supra* n. 9 at 147.
[39] *Id.* at SR-3.

given that athletes' reputations, and to some extent livelihoods, are at stake, the value of providing ample opportunity for targets to respond to the allegations underlying the investigation cannot be overstated.

Finding Corroboration

And finally, while there is no universal internal investigation plan, one universal rule holds true: search for corroboration.

This is especially the case for sports investigations, which run the gamut in terms of subject matter. Some address financial dealings of athletic officials and focus on the flow of funds and require forensic accounting analyses, while others focus on discrete events and witness observations/recollections. The Hunter Report, for example, centered on allegations of financial improprieties, so counsel retained an auditor to track the flow of money and provide financial analysis.[40] Others, like the Martin Report, focused on a series of isolated events that hinged on witness testimony and electronic communications.

Regardless of the specific investigation plan used, a key goal is to obtain corroborating evidence. Like presenting a case to a jury, one-witness cases are tough, as are pure document cases that have no "insider" or live witness to place those documents in context. And when the public and league are unable to judge the demeanor of the witnesses themselves, getting as much documentary and corroborative evidence is crucial. Such corroboration is all the more necessary in these types of investigations given the lack of subpoena power or legal ability to compel witness statements or testimony.

The Martin case is illustrative of the need to find documentary corroboration. There, lawyers were faced with a classic "he-said, she-said" situation—Martin discussed the impact Incognito's statements and behavior had on his psyche, whereas Incognito asserted that he never believed such statements had an effect on Martin, and in fact had no effect on Martin.[41] Much of the evidence was mixed—"not only did both linemen report that they enjoyed socializing together, the evidence

[40] *See* Hunter Report *supra* n. 29 at 3.
[41] *See* Martin Report *supra* n. 1 at 25-26.

showed that they often communicated in a vulgar manner."[42] Counsel also noted that Martin suffered from "mental health issues" and a "possible heightened sensitivity to insults and his unusual, 'bipolar' friendship with Incognito."[43] Counsel candidly acknowledged that they "struggle[d] with how to evaluate Martin's claims of harassment."[44]

In nonetheless concluding that Incognito bullied and verbally abused Martin, counsel pointed to numerous documents that corroborated Martin's versions of events, including a "notebook used to keep track of 'fines' the offensive lineman imposed on each other in their 'kangaroo court.'"[45] The notebook included a fine Incognito imposed on himself for "breaking Jmart" and a text message Incognito sent to other members of the Dolphins offensive line a week after Martin left the team. There, Incognito asked the linemen to destroy the "fine book," both of which suggested to counsel that Incognito knew what he was doing was wrong.[46]

Further, counsel highlighted "[c]ontemporaneous text messages that Martin sent to his parents and others months before he left the Dolphins—which have never before been made public."[47] In these text messages—sent before the investigation and while Martin was subject to the alleged harassment—Martin confessed to his parents that he was ashamed of his inability to confront the teammates who were bullying him, which he believed was a result of his attending private schools.[48] Martin repeatedly told his parents in text messages that the insults directed at him and about his mother and sister seriously upset him.[49] The lawyers concluded that "[w]ere [the texts between Martin and Incognito] the only available information for us to consider, it would be difficult to reach the conclusion that Martin truly felt harassed by Incognito and others . . . . The additional relevant information here includes Martin's contemporaneous text messages to his parents and the witness statements and documents showing that Player A and the Assistant Trainer were also harassed."[50]

---

[42] *Id.* at 2.
[43] *Id.* at 3.
[44] *Id.*
[45] *Id.*
[46] *Id.*
[47] *Id.* at 4.
[48] *See* Martin Report *supra* n. 1 at 15.
[49] *Id.* at 15-16.
[50] *Id.* at 37.

Another example is the MLB Report Investigation, in which the key witness, Kirk Radomski, a former clubhouse employee of the New York Mets, provided MLB with "copies of deposited checks that he retrieved from his banks, copies of some shipping labels or receipts, his telephone records for two years, and a copy of his address book in the form in which it was seized by federal agents when they executed a search warrant at his home."[51] Radomski also "provided detailed telephone records covering the period from June 2004 to June 2006. They show many calls made to telephone numbers that correspond to the numbers of Major League Baseball players. Radomski's address book also was provided to us in the form in which it existed when federal agents seized it during the execution of a search warrant at his home in December 2005. It includes many names and addresses of current and former Major League Baseball players. He also maintained copies of some delivery receipts"[52] These were key pieces of evidence that counsel used to corroborate Radomski's version of events—that he provided steroids to various major league baseball players.

Even in the Donaghy Investigation, while counsel "conducted approximately 200 interviews"—including speaking with fifty-seven referees who were employed by the League during a season in which Donaghy admitted to gambling on games he officiated—lawyers still "reviewed thousands of pages of documents that the League supplied at our request, including personnel files, statistical information, internal NBA documents and studies, and game video."[53] Prompted by press reports identifying over one hundred phone calls between Donaghy and fellow referee Scott Foster, counsel explored whether Foster was also gambling on basketball games.[54] Foster, however, provided benign explanations for the frequent phone calls, including that Donaghy was one of many referee friends with whom he would talk, which were confirmed by the times of the calls.[55] After comparing forensic evidence to Foster's statements, the Donaghy Report concluded that "[t]he report on Donaghy's phone records—when assessed in light of Foster's phone

---

[51] *See* MLB Report *supra* n. 9 SR-18.
[52] *See* MLB Report *supra* n. 9 140-41.
[53] *See* Donaghy Report *supra* n. 6 at 6.
[54] *Id.* at 28-29.
[55] *Id.* at 31-35.

records, Foster's friendship with Donaghy and the frequency with which Foster spoke to other referees—do not in our view raise concerns about [Foster's] integrity."[56]

In short, it is essential to outline multiple and separate work streams at the initiation of an internal investigation for sports organizations. While witness interviews are an obvious necessity, counsel should conduct searches of relevant custodians' electronic mailboxes; request pertinent financial records from the league and respective teams; and utilize consultants such as a forensic accounting firm, depending on the complexity of the issues. All of this evidence can help to corroborate or refute witnesses' versions of events.

Conclusion

If recent history is any guide, the sports industry will continue to provide white collar lawyers with some of the most challenging, high-profile investigations occurring today. This is not surprising given what is at stake when crises hit sports organizations; whether claims of corruption in officiating, embezzlement by high-ranking officials or hostile work environments, such allegations seize the public's attention and force sports organizations into a reactive mode. The volume of this work shows no signs of abating. The high-profile nature of these investigations demands retention of expert counsel, capable of resolving the complex issues described herein and managing the risks attendant to such investigations. Selecting the right counsel and employing and adapting the techniques described above will increase the likelihood of an effective, efficient, and credible sports investigation.

Key Takeaways

Key takeaways for lawyers conducting sports investigations include many of the same considerations associated with any white collar investigation. The importance of these takeaways, however, is heightened in a sports investigation, where the investigative report could become public and the report's conclusions could directly affect the investigation's subjects or targets.

---

[56] *Id.* at 35.

- *Autonomy:* It is essential for counsel to be given autonomy in conducting the investigation. Lawyers have routinely cited this factor in recent reports.
- *Full Support of Organizations:* This is a must. While all investigations—especially public ones—risk witnesses' lack of cooperation, having the league encourage cooperation goes a long way and helps allay witness concerns about reprisals within the league and the locker room.
- *Requests for Confidentiality:* Handling requests for confidentiality presents attorneys with a very fine line. While certain considerations may warrant maintaining confidentiality of witnesses—especially where there is a serious threat of reprisal—attributing statements to sources is an important aspect in assessing a report's findings. Where corroborative of other evidence, honoring such requests is a best practice as it encourages cooperation and helps protect percipient witnesses who are neither targets nor subjects of the investigation.
- *Seeking Corroborative Evidence:* Corroboration is key for any lawyer—on summary judgment, at trial, and in conducting an investigation. Given the lack of subpoena power and often competing witness statements, getting corroboration through documents or as many witness statements as possible is crucial.
- *Documenting the Investigation Plan and Any Limits Thereto:* To maintain the credibility of a report and place the conclusions in proper context, counsel should clearly document the steps taken in the course of the investigation and any limits to that investigation, including witnesses who refused to speak or documents that were unavailable.
- *Permitting Targets an Opportunity to Respond:* Like any adversary proceeding, counsel should permit the target to respond and provide his/her version of events. While targets of investigations may be reluctant to speak with investigators, or refuse to do so on advice of counsel, it is important to provide this opportunity for purposes of thoroughness and appearances of impartiality. Most importantly, the sharing of exculpatory evidence by a target will further the investigation's search for the truth.

***Alan Goudiss**, a partner in Shearman & Sterling LLP's Litigation Group, joined the firm in 1987 and became a partner in 1996. His practice includes a wide range of commercial, securities, corporate governance, and mergers and acquisitions litigation and advice. Mr. Goudiss is a member of the firm's Sports Group.*

***Christopher LaVigne** is counsel in the Litigation Group at Shearman & Sterling LLP. He previously served as a federal prosecutor with the US Attorney's Office for the Southern District of New York from 2005 to 2013. As a federal prosecutor, Mr. LaVigne was a member of the Securities and Commodities Fraud Task Force and earned a reputation as one of the Office's best trial lawyers.*

Mr. LaVigne's practice focuses on white collar criminal defense, regulatory enforcement defense, sports investigations, white collar investigations, and complex litigation matters. In 2014, Mr. LaVigne was named by Law360 *as one of five White Collar Rising Stars, which recognizes "attorneys under 40 whose legal accomplishments belie their age."*

Acknowledgment: *We gratefully acknowledge the contributions of Shearman & Sterling LLP associate Brian Calandra in drafting this chapter.*

Sports Law Litigation: Risk Management Considerations in Representing Recreation Providers and Defenses to Sports Injury Claims

Jill Haley Penwarden

Partner

Duane Morris LLP

ASPATORE

Introduction

In my practice, I represent a variety of recreation providers, including ski areas, golf courses, mountain bike parks, and rock climbing gyms. Prospectively, I provide risk management advice and services, such as drafting of liability releases and consulting on insurance, in order to protect my clients' interests.

When a participant is injured while participating in recreational activities and brings a lawsuit, I step in to defend my client. In a sports injury suit, a number of common issues arise. Depending on the nature of the claim and the allegations made, we assert the appropriate defenses on behalf of our client. In many cases, we are able to obtain a complete defense verdict, thanks to laws that can provide a complete defense based on the participant's inherent or express assumption of the risk of his or her activity. In other words, we are able to persuade the judge that the injured participant's case has no merit before it ever goes to a jury trial, based on a finding that the recreation provider is not legally responsible for the injury. The courts have recognized that it is impossible for recreation providers to eliminate the risks associated with participating in sports or other inherently dangerous activities. The courts are in many cases unwilling to impose liability on recreation providers for injuries such as those sustained because of inherent risks of the activity, such as when a skier loses control and hits a tree.

History of Sports Law Decisions and Statutory Law

Probably the most famous decision involving the concepts commonly applied to sports injuries is *Murphy v. Steeplechase Amusement Co.*, which involved an amusement park patron who was injured when he fell on a ride called "The Flopper," which was designed to throw patrons off their feet.[1] Judge Benjamin Cardozo (who went on to become a Supreme Court Justice in 1932) wrote a colorful opinion explaining why the plaintiff could not recover against the amusement park owners for his injuries:

> The antics of the clown are not the paces of the cloistered cleric…[the plaintiff] took the chance of a like fate, with

[1] *Murphy v. Steeplechase Amusement Co.*, 250 N.Y. 479, 166 N.E. 173 (1929).

> whatever damage to his body might ensue from such a fall. The timorous may stay at home.[2]

Several decades later, a skier in Vermont was injured when her ski struck a buried tree stump under the snow surface in an open run. In *Wright v. Mt. Mansfield Lift, Inc.*, 96 F.Supp. 786 (D.Vt. 1951), the court granted summary judgment for the defendant ski area operator, stating that "one who takes part in such a sport accepts the dangers that inhere in it so far as they are obvious and necessary."[3]

But then in 1978 the Vermont Supreme Court limited the application of the inherent danger rule in *Sunday v. Stratton Corp.*, 390 A.2d 398 (1978).[4] In that case, the plaintiff skier was paralyzed in an injury caused by his ski catching on a bush. The court in *Sunday* held the ski area to a duty of reasonable care—the same rule of ordinary care that all business owners owe to visitors—and upheld the jury's verdict that the ski area was negligent for failing to remove the bush.

Following the *Sunday* decision, a number of state legislatures enacted ski safety legislation. Most of these statutes provide recognition of the inherent risks of the sport, and set forth duties for ski area operators to follow.[5] Some states have enacted similar legislation pertaining to other sports, such as horseback riding.[6] A wide variety of recreational activities have been recognized as having inherent risks, including touch football, waterskiing, sailing, whitewater rafting, rock climbing, and judo, to name a few.[7]

In recent years, the California courts have recognized (as the court originally recognized in *Murphy v. Steeplechase, supra*, 166 N.E. 173) that the concept of primary assumption of risk applies not only to activities

---

[2] *Id.* at 174.

[3] *Wright v. Mt. Mansfield Lift, Inc.*, 96 F. Supp. 786 (D. Vt. 1951).

[4] *Id.* at 791.

[5] *See, e.g.*, Colorado's Ski Safety Act of 1979, codified at Colo. Rev. Stat. §§ 33-44-101-144 (West); Utah's Inherent Risks of Skiing Act, codified at Utah Code Ann. §§ 78-27-51-54 (2002 & Supp. 2007).

[6] *See, e.g.*, New Jersey's Equine Liability Statute, N.J. Stat. Ann. §§ 5:15-1-12.

[7] *Knight v. Jewett*, 3 Cal. 4th 296 (1992); *Ford v. Gouin*, 3 Cal. 4th 339 (1992); *Stimson v. Carlson*, 11 Cal. App. 4th 1201 (1992); *Ferrari v. Grand Canyon Dories*, 32 Cal. App. 4th 248 (1995); *Regents of Univ. of California v. Superior Court*, 41 Cal. App. 4th 1040 (1996); *Bushnell v. Japanese-Am. Religious & Cultural Ctr.*, 43 Cal.App.4th 525 (1996).

defined as "sports," but also to recreational activities with inherent risks, such as bumper car riding and walking into a smoldering fire at the Burning Man festival.[8]

Potential Claims

An injured sports participant can make a variety of claims against a recreation provider, depending on the degree of the claimed wrongful conduct. The most common allegation is of negligence, which is generally defined as the lack of ordinary care, or the failure of the recreation provider to act as a "reasonable person" would under the circumstances. Plaintiffs may also allege a higher degree of claimed wrongful conduct, such as gross negligence, recklessness, or willful misconduct.[9]

Defenses

In the context of sports law, a few common defenses may apply. These include primary (or implied) assumption of risk; express assumption of risk; and recreational immunity.

Primary Assumption of Risk

The primary, or implied, assumption of risk defense acknowledges that certain activities have inherent risks that cannot be eliminated without changing the nature of the activity, and therefore it would be inappropriate to hold a recreation provider liable for injuries resulting from those risks. For example, in *Knight v. Jewett*, the court acknowledged that:

> ...where, by virtue of the nature of the activity and the parties' relationship to the activity, the defendant owes no legal duty to protect the plaintiff from the particular risk of harm that caused the injury—the doctrine continues to operate as a complete bar to the plaintiff's recovery.[10]

[8] *Nalwa v. Cedar Fair, L.P.*, 55 Cal. 4th 1148 (2012); *Beninati v. Black Rock City, LLC*, 175 Cal. App. 4th 650 (2009).
[9] The plaintiff, however, cannot just make such allegations without a factual basis. If the plaintiff has no facts to support a claim of alleged wrongful conduct, it is subject to attack on procedural grounds such as a demurrer or motion to strike.
[10] *Knight v. Jewett*, 3 Cal. 4th 296, 313 (1992).

The elements that plaintiff must prove to make a negligence claim are: the existence of a duty to the injured person; the breach of that duty; causation of the injury; and resulting damages. The primary assumption of risk defense effectively negates the duty element of the alleged tort, because as a matter of law the defendant has no duty to eliminate, or protect participants from, risks that are inherent in the activity. The California Supreme Court recently clarified that a recreation provider or participant has no duty to *minimize* the inherent risks of an activity, but only the duty *not to increase* those risks.[11]

A coach or co-participant's legal duty to participants may be analyzed slightly differently than a recreation provider's duty. For example, in California, a coach or co-participant can be found liable only if he or she either intentionally injures another participant, or engages in conduct "so reckless as to be totally outside the range of the ordinary activity" involved in the sport.[12] The California courts have observed that there would be a chilling effect on vigorous participation in sports, or on coaching sports, to find liability for co-participants' negligence, because "in the heat of an active sporting event...a participant's normal energetic conduct often includes accidentally careless behavior..."[13]

If the defense of primary assumption of risk applies, the defendant can file a motion for summary judgment, or other procedural motion, asking the court to dismiss the plaintiff's case as a matter of law. If the defendant had no duty to protect the plaintiff from the risk he or she encountered, the defendant cannot be held liable for the injury.

Express Assumption of Risk

Liability releases can be used both to inform the participant about potential risks, and to protect the provider in the event of an injury. In cases where the participant is injured after signing a pre-injury release of liability, the defense of express assumption of risk often applies.

Liability releases have been recognized by the courts as barring a plaintiff's sports injury claim in many states, including Arkansas, California, Colorado,

---

[11] *Nalwa*, 55 Cal. 4th at 1161.
[12] *Cheong v. Antablin*, 16 Cal. 4th 1063, 1072 (1977).
[13] *Id.* at 1072; *see Kahn v. East Side Union H.S. Dist.*, 31 Cal. 4th 990 (2003).

Delaware, Florida, Georgia, Hawaii, Idaho, Illinois, Indiana, Iowa, Kansas, Kentucky, Maine, Maryland, Massachusetts, Michigan, Minnesota, Mississippi, Missouri, Nebraska, Nevada, New Hampshire, New Jersey, New Mexico, Ohio, Oklahoma, Oregon, Pennsylvania, Rhode Island, South Carolina, South Dakota, Tennessee, Texas, Washington, and Wyoming.[14]

On the other hand, a few states have prohibited the use of recreational releases, either by judicial pronouncement or by statute, including Louisiana, Montana, Utah, Vermont, and Virginia.[15]

Even in states that generally recognize pre-injury releases as valid, in some cases a particular release may be struck down as inadequately worded to cover the claim, or on public policy grounds. However, one plaintiff's attempt in California to have pre-injury releases invalidated under unfair competition laws or as against public policy was rejected on the basis that

---

[14] *Van Weire v. Styles*, 2013 Ark. App. 208 (2013); *Knight v. Jewett*, 3 Cal.4th 296 (1992); *Messer v. Hi Country Stables Corp.*, No. 11-CV-01500-WJM-MJW, 2013 WL 93183 (D. Colo. Jan. 8, 2013); *Slowe v. Pike Creek Court Club, Inc.*, CIV.A. 08C-08-029PLA, 2008 WL 5115035 (Del. Super. Dec. 4, 2008); *Gilette v. All Pro Sports, LLC*, 5D12-1527, 2014 WL 258762 (Fla. Dist. Ct. App. Jan. 24, 2014) (2014); *Herren v. Sucher*, 325 Ga. App. 219, 750 S.E.2d 430 (2013), reconsideration denied (Dec. 3, 2013); *Fujimoto v. Au*, 95 Haw. 116, 19 P.3d 699 (2001); *Salinas v. Vierstra*, 107 Idaho 984 (1985); *Cox v. U.S. Fitness, LLC*, 2013 IL App (1st) 122442 (2013); *Heck v. Robey*, 659 N.E.2d 498 (Ind. 1995); *Hysell v. Iowa Pub. Serv. Co.*, 534 F.2d 775 (8th Cir. 1876); *New Hampshire Ins. Co. v. Fox Midwest Theatres, Inc.*, 203 Kan. 720 (1969); *Cumberland Valley Contractors, Inc. v. Bell Cnty. Coal Corp.*, 238 S.W.3d 644 (2007); *Lloyd v. Sugarloaf Mountain Corp.*, 833 A.2d 1 (2003); *Adloo v. H.T. Brown Real Estate, Inc.*, 344 Md. 254 (1996); *Lee v. Allied Sports Associates, Inc.*, 349 Mass. 544 (1965); *Cole v. Ladbroke Racing Michigan, Inc.*, 614 N.W.2d 169 (2000); *Schlobohm v. Spa Petite, Inc.*, 326 N.W.2d 920 (Minn. 1982); *Holmes v. Multimedia KSDK, Inc.*, 395 S.W.3d 557 (Mo. Ct. App. 2013); *New Light Co. Inc. v. Wells Fargo Alarm Servs. Div. of Baker Protective Servs., Inc.*, 525 N.W.2d 25 (1994); *Miller v. A & R Joint Venture*, 97 Nev. 580 (1981); *Dean v. MacDonald*, 147 N.H 263 (2001); *Knorr v. Smeal*, 178 N.J. 169 (2003); *Sw. Pub. Serv. Co. v. Artesia Alfalfa Grower's Ass'n*, 67 N.M. 108 (1960); *Hague v. Summit Acres Skilled Nursing & Rehab.*, 2010-Ohio-6404 (Ohio App. 2010); *Schmidt v. U.S.*, 912 P.2d 871 (1996); *Bagley v. Mt. Bachelor, Inc.*, 310 P.3d 692 (Or. App. 2013); *Tayar v. Camelback Ski Corp., Inc.*, 616 Pa. 385, 47 A.3d 1190 (2012); *Corrente v. Conforti & Eisele Co., Inc.*, 468 A.2d 920 (R.I. 1983); *Fisher v. Stevens*, 355 S.C. 290 (Ct. App. 2003); *Paterek v. 6600 Ltd.*, 465 N.W.2d 342 (1990); *Perez v. McConkey*, 872 S.W.2d 897 (Tenn. 1994); *Van Voris v. Team Chop Shop, LLC*, 402 S.W.3d 915 (Tex. App. 2013); *Johnson v. Spokane to Sandpoint, LLC*, 176 Wash. App. 453, 309 P.3d 528 (2013); *Milligan v. Big Valley Corp.*, 754 P.2d 1063 (Wyo. 1988).

[15] La. Civ. Code Ann. art. 2004 (2011); Mont. Code Ann. § 28-2-702; *Rothstein v. Snowbird Corp.*, 2007 UT 96, 175 P.3d 560 (2007); *Hiett v. Lake Bancroft Cmty. Ass'n*, 244 Va. 191, 418 S.E.2d 894 (1992); *Dalury v. S-K-I, Ltd.*, 164 Vt. 329, 670 A.2d 795 (1995).

recreational releases do not implicate a service of "great importance" or practical necessity to the public, and because the plaintiff has a choice to recreate elsewhere or in other ways without signing a release agreement.[16]

Considerations in Drafting a Liability Release

One of the best defenses to a sports law claim may be that the injured party has signed a pre-injury release of liability. However, this defense requires that, before any claim arises, the injured party has signed an appropriate release agreement that will be upheld to legally bar the claim.

A crucial mistake that many recreation providers make is to use either an outdated release (perhaps drafted or reviewed by a lawyer many years ago, but never updated) or to "borrow" a release from some other source, whether an online source or another similar business. A release should be tailored to the particular provider, the activity and its risks, and reviewed frequently (ideally annually) by an attorney familiar with this area of law and any changes in the law that may have occurred. Every year, new court decisions and statutes shape the law that applies to releases, and a failure to bring release agreements up to date may cause a business to rely on a liability release that turns out to be unenforceable.

A Release Must Be Valid Under State Law

In drafting a release, the drafter must think about what law will apply. The law that applies to releases of liability varies from state to state.

Generally, recreation providers specify in their releases that the law of their home state will apply. Before relying on a release for liability protection, however, the provider must understand whether its state will view it as valid. Many states have case law indicating that releases of liability for recreational activities are valid and do not violate public policy. As discussed above, however, some states may hold pre-injury liability releases to be unenforceable. In those states, the defense of express assumption of risk may not be available.

Further, some states may not allow parents or guardians to sign liability releases on behalf of their minor children. In specifying what law will

[16] *Olsen v. Breeze, Inc.*, 48 Cal. App. 4th 608 (1996).

apply, be sure you know that the state you choose will uphold the release; these laws change frequently. For example, in *Cooper v. Aspen Skiing Company*, the Colorado Supreme Court addressed the application of liability releases to claims by minors.[17] In that case, seventeen-year-old ski racer David Cooper lost control and struck a tree while training on a race. He suffered severe injuries, including blindness. Cooper's mother had signed a pre-injury release on his behalf at the beginning of that ski season. The Colorado Supreme Court addressed the question of whether Colorado's public policy allowed parents to contractually release their child's future claims for injury caused by negligence, and concluded that Colorado law precluded parents from releasing a child's prospective claims. The next year, in 2003, the Colorado legislature passed Colorado Senate Bill 253, overruling the holding of *Cooper v. Aspen*, and making it legal for parents to waive minors' claims.[18]

In Utah, the law changed significantly over two decisions within a single year. In *Berry v. Greater Park City Co.*, the court held that, where a participant was injured in a skier cross race, his claim against the ski area was barred by a release agreement he had signed.[19] But then in *Rothstein v. Snowbird Corp.*, the Utah Supreme Court held that, under the language of Utah's Inherent Risks of Skiing Act, enforcing liability releases was contrary to Utah's public policy, and as a result holding the use of liability releases invalid.[20]

Before relying on releases of liability to reduce your risk as a provider, be sure to know if these releases will be upheld in general, or in specific circumstances.

A Release Must Be Properly Worded

Some states generally uphold releases but have refused to apply particular releases to bar a claim based on the wording of the release. For example, a court may find that a release does not apply, on the basis that the release was void under the circumstances, or did not unambiguously cover the risk that the injured party encountered.

---

[17] *Cooper v. Aspen Skiing Company*, 48 P.3d 1229 (Colo. 2002).
[18] S.B. 253 (Co. 2003).
[19] *Berry v. Greater Park City Co.*, 2007 UT 87, ¶12 (2007).
[20] *Rothstein v. Snowbird Corp*, 2007 UT 96, ¶20 (2007).

For example, in *Huverserian v. Catalina SCUBA Luv, Inc.*, a diver ran out of air while scuba diving with rented equipment, and died.[21] His family sued the equipment rental company, which asserted the defense that the decedent's liability release barred the claim. Unfortunately for the defendant, the title of the form release was "Equipment rental agreement, liability release and assumption of risk of scuba and snorkel gear for boat dives or multiple day rentals." Because the decedent was not using the equipment for a boat dive and requested only a single-day rental, the California Court of Appeal held that it did not apply to bar his heirs' claims.[22] "[A] person renting equipment for a single day, not to be used on a boat dive, would read the emphasized language and reasonably determine that it did not apply to him or her, and conclude that by signing the agreement, he or she had only agreed to the rental terms with no release of liability intended."[23] Had the equipment rental company used a release agreement that expressly applied to *all* equipment rentals, the release might well have barred the claim.

On the other hand, a properly drafted release can provide a complete defense to a sports law claim.

In *Gregorie v. Alpine Meadows Ski Corp.*, a snowboarder suffered fatal injuries when she slipped while hiking to expert terrain, fell over a rock outcropping, and came to rest outside the ski area boundary.[24] Gregorie had signed a liability release for "any and all risk of injury or death which may be associated with [her] participation in the sports of skiing and snowboarding and the use of the facilities at Alpine, including…skiing or snowboarding beyond the ski area boundaries…" The plaintiffs, Gregorie's parents, contended that the liability release was contrary to public policy and/or that Alpine had misled her as to the "backcountry" nature of the area where she was traveling. The court rejected these claims, stating that "Although not specifically included in the release, it is apparent that a skier or snowboarder while hiking on a steep slope could slip, fall and experience an uncontrollable slide…The release made Gregorie aware that skiing and

---

[21] *Huverserian v. Catalina Scuba Luv, Inc.*, 184 Cal. App. 4th 1462 (2010).
[22] *Id.* at 1469.
[23] *Id.*
[24] *Gregorie v. Alpine Meadows Ski Corp.*, CIV. S-08-259 LKK/DA, 2009 WL 2425960 (E.D. Cal. Aug. 7, 2009).

snowboarding at Alpine posed the risk of injury or death…." The court therefore granted summary judgment for the ski area defendants based on the release (in addition to primary assumption of risk).[25]

A California court has acknowledged the challenges of drafting a "perfect" release agreement:

> Drafters of releases always face the problem of steering between the Scylla of simplicity and the Charybdis of completeness. Apparently no release is immune from attack. If short and to the point, a release will be challenged as failing to mention the particular risk which caused a plaintiff's injury or as insufficiently comprehensive. It will be attacked as totally ineffective if a key word is placed in the caption for emphasis but not repeated in the text, or if, despite unambiguous language, the word "negligence" is not used…
>
> To be effective a release need not achieve perfection; only on Draftsman's Olympus is it feasible to combine the elegance of a trust indenture with the brevity of a stop sign… It suffices that a release be clear, unambiguous, and explicit, and that it express an agreement not to hold the released party liable for negligence.[26]

While releases may never be able to be "perfectly" drafted, it is important to consider the options of listing all of the potential risks, versus describing a general category of risks (i.e. "all risks associated with bicycle riding"). The best release will likely strike a balance between the two extremes.

Release Language Should Be Conspicuous

The courts have struck down releases for not being "conspicuous" enough. A judge scrutinizing a release will likely want to see that the release of liability provisions would have been readily apparent to the signer, not

[25] *Id.* at *20.
[26] *Nat'l & Internat. Bhd. of Street Racers, Inc. v. Superior Court*, 215 Cal. App. 3d 934, 937-38 (1990) [internal citations omitted].

buried in small print in the middle of unrelated text. An explanatory title, perhaps in addition to an additional statement before the signature line, can help draw attention to the significance of the document.

While there is often a desire to save space by using smaller fonts, the drafter should not succumb to the temptation to use tiny print to fit a lengthy agreement onto one page for convenience's sake. There is no hard-and-fast "rule" about what type size to use, although generally ten-point font should be considered large enough. (Some courts have upheld releases using smaller font sizes, but it is better to be safe than sorry.) The drafter should also consider the placement of the release language within the document, and consider selectively using bold type and capital letters to call attention to key provisions. The drafter should also attempt to use "plain English" non-legal language as much as possible. It is preferable (and may be required under state law) to specify that the participant is releasing liability for the released parties' alleged negligence. Some states may require the release agreement to specify that it is not, however, an attempt to waive responsibility for gross negligence or other forms of alleged aggravated misconduct. Be sure to consider the applicable state law in drafting release language.

Include All Potential Defendants

It is important to be comprehensive as to which parties should be listed in the release. The drafter should think about who might be target defendants in the event of a claim. These might include the recreation provider, its affiliated entities, landowners, event promoters, sponsors, and the like. Catchall categories (i.e., "[provider's] owners, investors, officers, directors, employees," etc.) can be used in addition as well. Recreation providers operating on state or federal land may also be required to list those governmental entities as released parties.

Recreational Immunity

Finally, if the injured sports participant was recreating on a property owner's land without paying a fee, recreational immunity may apply. All states have enacted statutory provisions providing immunity to landowners for recreational injuries on their property. These statutes are intended to encourage landowners to allow the public to use their land for recreational purposes.[27] For example, California Civil Code Section 846 provides that:

> An owner of any estate or any other interest in real property, whether possessory or nonpossessory, owes no duty of care to keep the premises safe for entry or use by others for any recreational purpose or to give any warning of hazardous conditions, uses of, structure, or activities on such premises to persons entering for such purpose....[28]

Recreational immunity statutes may provide a complete defense where the injured party was using land for recreation without paying a fee. Examples of lawsuits where recreational immunity has been found to provide a complete defense to a claim have involved injuries resulting from hiking, swimming, picnicking, driving, bicycling, and motorcycle riding on federal land; children playing on farm equipment on private land; attending a free air show; sledding on sand dunes; retrieval of a kite from power lines; and skateboarding in a friend's driveway.

Any recreational provider or landowner facing a claim should consider whether the injured party paid a fee to participate in the activity, and if not, whether recreational immunity may apply.

Special Event Considerations

Many liability issues arise in connection with special events, such as an annual "mud run" or 5K race. It is important for the event organizers to coordinate effectively regarding liability issues.

First, the event organizers should collectively make sure that the participants sign an up-to-date release of liability listing all potential target defendants. These include the promoter, landowners, course designers and other vendors, and all other businesses involved in hosting or organizing the event.

---

[27] *See* Terence J. Centner, *Revising State Recreational Use Statutes to Assist Private Property Owners and Providers of Outdoor Recreational Activities*, 9 BUFFALO ENVT'L L. J. 1 (2001).
[28] Cal. Civ. Code § 846 (West).

Further, well in advance of the race, the involved parties should make sure to resolve liability and insurance-related issues such as whether one party will indemnify the other, how much insurance coverage will be required, who will provider workers' compensation insurance for staff, which party's insurance coverage will be primary in the event of a claim, and ensure that there are no coverage exclusions which would undermine coverage in the event of an injury to a participant, spectator, or employee. Recreation providers should consider (and their insurers may require) having an event promoter provide a certificate of insurance naming the appropriate parties as additional insureds, well in advance of the event. Do not be caught in the uncomfortable situation of learning that the promoter has inadequate or no insurance on the eve of the event, well after the event has already been promoted to the public.

The parties will also need to clarify (preferably in a written agreement) their respective roles in advance of the event. Examples include who will be responsible for course design, whose employees will set up and break down the course, who has authority to close the course in the event of a potential safety hazard (for example, an electrical storm), and who will provide any needed personnel to address safety issues on the course.

The death of participant Avishek Sengupta at a Tough Mudder event in April 2013 provides a cautionary tale. Sengupta was participating in the 2013 Mid-Atlantic Tough Mudder event in Maryland with five teammates when he jumped from a fifteen-foot-high platform into a pool of muddy water at an obstacle called "Walk the Plank." After Sengupta jumped into the pool, which was fifteen feet deep and forty feet wide, he did not surface. Although it is unclear what happened, another participant may have jumped on top of him. His teammates contend that, despite their exhortations to lifeguards and a rescue diver to act, the rescue diver did not enter the water for several minutes, the rescue diver wasted time yelling at other participants and initially entered the water without proper equipment, and that Sengupta was not brought to the surface until more than eight minutes had elapsed.[29] Sengupta later died of his injuries. Although Tough Mudder has not commented in the media on the episode, most likely due to the possibility of a lawsuit by Sengupta's family, some have suggested that

---

[29] Outside Magazine, *Death at Tough Mudder*, (uploaded Dec. 10, 2013), *available at* www.youtube.com/watch?v=Gs0gYU7uBcE.

lack of clear communication or a clear chain of command between Tough Mudder and Amphibious Medics, the company that employed the diver in question, could have led to the delay in attempting to rescue Sengupta.

Whatever its cause, Sengupta's accident illustrates the importance of pre-event coordination so that there is no confusion between the organizers and their employees as to what to do in the event of an accident or serious injury. *Outside Magazine* reports that Tough Mudder is reviewing its procedures in the wake of this incident.[30] Event organizers should consider the need to have emergency medical personnel or other emergency staff standing by in case the need arises, to eliminate any potential delays in response and treatment.

Event hosts and organizers should do their best to anticipate and prepare for worst-case scenarios *before* they occur. They should spend time thinking about the risks and the respective roles of all involved parties in responding to injuries or issues that may occur (such as a participant failing to surface in a water feature) or how to address those potential risks before an injury occurs (such as requiring participants to jump one at a time, or having a rescue diver in full gear standing by in the event of an incident, for example). It is impossible to eliminate the risks associated with these types of activities, but time spent thinking about how to address them will be time well spent.

Consider scheduling a meeting with the event promoter, operational personnel, marketing personnel, and legal counsel well in advance of the event to discuss and work through these issues. The recreation provider should be sure to maintain frequent communication between all departments or employees who are working on the event to ensure that things go as smoothly as possible and potential problems are not uncovered on the eve of the event or, even worse, in the course of the event.

Conclusion

The courts in most states have recognized that certain activities have inherent risks that cannot be eliminated without fundamentally changing the sport.

---

[30] Elliott D. Woods, *A Death at Tough Mudder*, OUTSIDE MAGAZINE, (Dec. 2, 2013), *available at* http://www.outsideonline.com/outdoor-adventure/multisport/Man-Under-Avishek-Sengupta-Tough-Mudder-Death.html.

Many states have also recognized that, in the context of recreational activities, the parties can freely contract to allocate the risks, through a liability release. Finally, all states have enacted legislation protecting landowners from suits by persons using their land for recreational purposes. Indeed, the costs of insurance and defending participant lawsuits might be prohibitive if the courts fail to recognize these concepts.

Key Takeaways

- When a sports participant is injured, primary assumption of risk may provide a complete defense if the injury resulted from an inherent risk of the activity.
- When a sports participant is injured, express assumption of risk may provide a complete defense if the participant signed a release of liability.
- Take care in drafting a liability release. Do not use an outdated liability release or "borrow" a release from some other source. A release should be tailored to the particular provider, the activity, its risks, the applicable law, list all potential target defendants, and be reviewed periodically by an attorney familiar with this area of law and any changes in the law that may have occurred.
- Examine whether the injured party paid a fee to participate in the activity, and if not, whether recreational immunity may apply. Encourage event organizers to collectively make sure that the participants sign an up-to-date release of liability listing all potential target defendants.
- When putting on special events, recreation providers should proactively address questions of potential risk, insurance and indemnity issues, allocation of risks and responsibilities, and other liability considerations well in advance of the event.

Jill Haley Penwarden is a partner with the Lake Tahoe office of Duane Morris LLP, a full-service international law firm. She represents a wide variety of sports and recreation providers, including ski resorts, mountain bike parks, golf courses, outdoor outfitters, climbing gyms, resort communities, and hotel properties, in the California state and federal courts. In addition to defending recreation providers in litigation, Ms. Penwarden provides proactive risk management advice to her clients.

Legal Issues Surrounding the Olympic Games and Other Sporting Events Entering the 21st Century

Kelly Charles Crabb

Partner

Sheppard Mullin Richter & Hampton LLP

ASPATORE

Introduction

I began my career working at a large firm in New York after I graduated from Columbia Law School in 1984. I spent some time in Japan when I was younger, where I learned Japanese and, like many people, I fell in love with the country. This enabled me to start out at my firm working in corporate matters related to Japanese transactions. In due course, this led me to the world of entertainment. One of our clients, a Japanese television company, provided me with the opportunity to work with Paul McCartney and his brother-in-law, John Eastman—basically, I was lucky enough to start my entertainment career representing one of the Beatles.

In 1990, my firm transferred me to Los Angeles, where the Japanese were heavily investing in intellectual property. Japan had a tax law that allowed people to depreciate any IP investments on a two-year schedule. They would form investment funds to buy, for example, the copyright of various US movies, the distribution rights to which would be "leased" (technically, licensed) back to the motion picture studio that produced the movies. After a certain period of time (for example, after the movie's traditional life cycle), the motion picture studio would have the right to buy back the copyright of the movies for a pre-negotiated, often nominal, price. This film financing boom also lead to an increase of Japanese activity generally in the motion picture industry—I worked on many rights acquisition transactions, develop and production deals. This experience allowed me to build up a reputation as an entertainment lawyer generally and I proceeded to work on more film projects, including the *Ali* movie, starring Will Smith, among others.

Around 1996, I was approached by a former NFL player and a promoter with an idea. He and his partner had a relationship with NBA star, Charles Barkley, and proposed to play a series of exhibition games in Japan. I was able to put together a deal with the NBA and a Japanese promoter. Eventually, we arranged for fourteen high-level NBA players to take part in a two-night exhibition at the Tokyo Dome. It was a huge success with sellout crowds and television coverage. This was my first foray into sports law. It involved a lot of negotiation with the NBA and the players' union, but it was a lot of fun. After that, I ended up working with Charles Barkley and even Michael Jordan on some commercial endorsement deals as well.

About a year after this, I received a call from a friend from law school who was then general counsel of the Salt Lake City Olympic Committee. He asked me to look into a music contract he had been working on. The contract involved a tricky copyright related matter and I was able to advise him on that. After this, the committee began to hire me to do other things, and I started working with them on a variety of things primarily related to the opening and closing ceremonies. In 2001, when Beijing won its bid to host the 2008 Olympic Games, I had a chance meeting in Los Angeles with one of my partners from Beijing and I suggested to him that we should go after the Beijing Organizing Committee to represent them. His comment to me was, "What do they need lawyers for?" Eventually, I persuaded him and my other colleagues in China that there was an important role for lawyers related to the entertainment (opening and closing ceremonies) and commercial (tickets, trademark licensing, sponsorships, and broadcasting) aspects of the Olympic Games. As I understand it, we were one of over a hundred firms that wanted to get the work in Beijing; we were fortunate enough to win the bid. I was privileged to chair a group of attorneys at my firm related to the Beijing Olympics work. We represented the committee for over six years. I traveled to Beijing over thirty times, went to Switzerland twice, and worked regularly on the sponsorship, licensing, broadcasting, ticketing, and entertainment matters of the Beijing Games, among other things.

Being the lawyers for the Beijing Olympic Committee led to other opportunities. We were able to represent the NBA in several transactions in China. One of these matters was a "reality show" where young Chinese athletes were allowed to compete to be on "all-star" teams that would compete on television. We also represented Major League Baseball in an interesting China deal aimed at discovering and developing native Chinese baseball talent. These matters involved publicity rights, broadcasting rights, and a host of other issues common to commercial sports in an international setting.

Sports Commerce and Sports Law Through the Years

Sports law is essentially made up of five areas—entertainment law, plus four areas of commerce: ticketing, licensing, sponsorships, and broadcasting. The ultimate objective of sports promotion is for people to either buy tickets to go see the sporting event live or, nowadays, sit in front of their television and watch it, and, in the process, become interested enough to buy paraphernalia that is branded with the logos and other symbols of the teams they like (not to mention the products of the companies that sponsor the live events and broadcasts). People will do that if they are entertained. So, promoters of sporting events pay attention to the pageantry of sports—especially with Olympic events where the most watched segments are the opening and closing ceremonies. There are a plethora of legal issues related to all of this.

The commerce side of sports goes a long ways back. The very first modern Olympics was held in Athens in 1896—they did not have any broadcasting or sponsors, but they sold tickets to the games, took donations, and sold merchandise in the form of pins and other memorabilia. In many ways, not much has changed in the last century. Complications have come hand-in-hand with technological advances in most facets of the industry. For example, when tickets are sold internationally, there are privacy laws in virtually all nations related to storing names in a database that must be complied with. Merchandising involves the protection and licensing of special trademarks associated with the events and team participants. Sponsorship deals related to large sporting events and professional sports franchises structured within a large and complex master plan provides international versus local rights, product category exclusivity, tiers of benefits, and other matters, such as the payment of sponsorship fees with value in kind (VIK). The modern broadcasting deals, the most lucrative of all, are characterized by territorial exclusivity and a host of services and rights provisions related to such matters as camera positions, space at the broadcasting center, even catering.

Broadcasting is a young industry in that it has only been around since the dawn of radio and television, but has undergone many changes over the years. In the Olympic world, a recent change, since the Beijing Olympics, is that the organizing committee is no longer a party to the broadcast rights agreements. In Beijing, and the Olympics prior, the broadcast agreements involved three parties—the International Olympic Committee (IOC), the rights holder (for example, NBC in the United States), and the organizing committee. The organizing committee provided services and allocated the broadcasting resources among the many rights holders. For example, each broadcaster is entitled to a place in the International Broadcast Center, hotel accommodations, transportation and parking privileges, accreditation for its personnel, and other privileges related to the massive endeavor of transmitting the images and stories of the Olympics back home. Some of the larger rights holders (again, for example, NBC) are entitled to their own camera positions within the venues. Since sorting all of this out requires detailed logistical planning, the organizing committee—that actually provides the services and administrates the facilities—was a party to the broadcasting agreement and participated in the negotiations. After Beijing, the organizing committee was no longer a party. The IOC enters into an agreement with each of the rights holders and a separate agreement with the organizing committee. The IOC determines how to allocate the services and accommodation, in consultation with the organizing committee.

Another interesting issue that has arisen in the more recent era has to do with "ambush marketing." Sponsors of large athletic events pay a lot of money to associate with the given sporting event or franchise. In the Olympic Movement, for example, sponsors enjoy being the "exclusive" sponsor in a certain product category—for example, Coca-Cola for beverages, McDonald's for food, Panasonic for television sets, Samsung for cell phones, etc. Competitors of these "official" sponsors have, from time to time, tried various schemes to create the impression that they were associated with the Olympics or other sporting events without, of course, paying the sponsorship fee. There have been examples of airplanes dragging a non-sponsor's banner over a venue, advertisements placed within view of the official venues, and other clever methods far too numerous to mention. These ambush techniques are not popular, to say the least, with the official sponsors. Starting with the Vancouver and London Games, the IOC started to impose an obligation in the Host City Contract—the agreement that every Host City and National Olympic Committee must sign upon being awarded the right to host the Olympic Games—that statutory protections against ambush marketing must be enacted in the municipality and even the national government. This could become a significant legal issue when the United States is next elected to host an Olympic Games due to notions of and cases dealing with commercial free speech.

Generally, the IOC is very good at preparing host cities for the legal issues that come up along the way. They have a great deal of experience and are able to implement solutions due to lessons learned at past Olympic venues.

The Olympic Movement has certain guiding principles, such as "clean venue," which further its commercial viability. Advertising is prohibited within venues (unlike the World Cup, for example) and host cities are required to secure the rights to billboards and advertising rights near venues and major transportation hubs in order to protect the official sponsors. The issue of ambush marketing will likely persist. There is a surprising lack of court activity related to this issue, probably because the IOC and other major sports franchises do not want to risk an adverse legal precedent. Rather, they continue to apply pressure where they can to protect the official sponsors. The IOC must feel confident it will be able to continue to do so—just recently it announced a dramatic increase in the price of a worldwide sponsorship.

The Olympic Host City Contract

In the Olympic Movement, the foundation documents are the Olympic Charter and the Host City Contract. Each city that hopes to host an Olympic Games must spend substantial sums of money simply to make the various assessments required. There are endless inspections by the IOC, which looks into such matters as transportation, security, accommodations, and the economic and environmental impact of the Games. At the end of the process, the winner must sign the Host City Contract within minutes of the announcement. Of course, this is not a surprise. The IOC sends out the contract before the bids are finalized in order for the bidders to have an opportunity to review its provisions. Some negotiations might be possible, but by in large the contract will be as originally drafted.

The Host City Contract is signed by the host city (i.e., the municipal government) and the National Olympic Committee (each nation has one), and is endorsed by the host nation. At this point in time, the IOC has a lot of contract leverage, as cities and nations appear willing to make the expenditures needed to host the Games. This is why the IOC has been able to require changes in national laws related to the protection of Olympic marks and, more recently, against ambush marketing. For example, it was rumored that the IOC was concerned about China's ability to prevent counterfeit goods in connection with the Beijing Games. Ultimately, however, the city of Beijing and the national government both enacted trademark protection statutes specifically dealing with Olympic trademarks and did aggressively pursue counterfeiters of Olympic and Games merchandise.

The terms of the Host City Contract involve, among others, the following primary issues:

- Establishment of the organizing committee and its responsibilities
- Responsibility for the marketing of the Games
- Mandates related to transportation, security, accommodations, and environmental protection
- Compliance with the technical requirements of each sport and the organization of the sports program
- Organization of the cultural program
- Organization of the ceremonies and the Torch Relay
- Rules related to ticketing, merchandise licensing, sponsorships, and broadcasting
- Protection of Olympic symbols and obligation to assign all intellectual property associated with the Games to the IOC
- Obligations related to the Paralympic Games
- Accreditation of athletes

Legal Issues Surrounding Ticketing

The ticketing process for an Olympic Games usually involves a master agreement with an established ticket vendor that has both experience and a broad geographical reach. Professional sports franchises, which perform at the same venues year after year, may develop their own ticketing organization, but many still use outside vendors. The advent of the Internet has had an impact on the way tickets are sold. For international events, such as the Olympic Games, there are extensive privacy issues that need to be addressed as well. Privacy issues arise, because it is necessary to store the name, address, and other personal information about the ticket purchaser in a database. Privacy laws, especially in the European Union, can be very strict—and an organizing committee typically will engage attorneys with privacy law compliance expertise to assist. The ticket itself is a contract between the organizing committee and the ticket holder. The terms on the back usually contain provisions related to the conduct of the ticketholder—what the holder can bring into the venue, limits on liability and so forth. The ticket often only contains the short form of the contract but also refers to a longer form online. The ticket can cover, for example, ambush marketing concerns. During the 2006 FIFA World Cup, spectators wearing orange *leeuwenhosen* (overalls) containing the brand name of a competitor of the official sponsor, Budweiser, were ordered by officials in Stuttgart to either leave the venue or disrobe based on language in the ticket against wearing branded apparel. Many of the die-hard Dutch supporters watched the game in their underwear. Likewise, the ticket can contain restrictions on recording equipment (such as video cameras) and dangerous items. Tickets also provide for the right of the organizer (or organizer's broadcast rights holder) to film ticket holders, thereby providing a contractual basis for including such person's image on film.

Legal Issues Surrounding Licensing

Licensing (as well as sponsorships, explored below) in a sports context rests on the foundation of trademark law. The word "Olympics" (as applied to the modern international sports festival of the modern era) and the five-ring Olympic symbol have, over the years, acquired tremendous good will. People associate the Olympic Games with the excitement of international competition and with the altruistic ideals of hard work, peaceful competition among nations, and the glory of individual and team accomplishment. This good will gives rise on the part of many people to want to be associated with the Games—to own some item that embodies that good will. Hats, T-shirts, plates, key chains, posters, mascots, and a wide variety of other items branded with the Olympic or Games trademarks are sold in vast quantities to fans at the Games and around the world.

The IOC and, for that matter, all major sports franchises, and even colleges, clubs, and other sports organizations, promote their good will through trademarks and trade names. Trademarks are protected by national laws through registration and, in the United States, for example, use. The IOC, for example, is aggressive in registering each official Games symbol in all developed nations in all available classes. Up until the Salt Lake City 2002 Winter Games, the IOC delegated the responsibility of registering Games-related trademarks to the organizing committees. Now, however, the task is performed by the IOC itself. The NBA, NFL, and MLB also diligently register the name and symbol of each of their respective teams, as well as certain other "league" symbols and names.

The right of a third party manufacturer to use any of these registered trademarks is the subject of an official license. Selling branded goods without a license is trademark infringement, and organizing committees, national committees, and the IOC spend much time and effort to stop such counterfeiting activities. It is important to protect the official licensees by going after counterfeiters. In Salt Lake City, the organizing committee, realizing that it could not sue the infringer, decided to handpick easy cases to win and heavily publicize them in order to scare anyone else from selling counterfeit goods. They went after mom-and-pop shops in the city and it was covered extensively in the newspapers. In Beijing, they did the same thing but on a much greater scale—they had hundreds of cases in the months leading up to it, and were able to stay on top of the counterfeit products.

Legal Issues Surrounding Sponsorship Agreements

Sports-related sponsorships are prevalent at all levels, and are based on the same "good will" discussed above. Sponsors pay money for the right to be associated with that good will. There is proven value in being the "official sponsor" of an Olympic Games, an Olympic team, the NBA, NFL, MLB, FIFA or the NHL, to name a few. As noted above, in the Olympic Movement, the IOC sells about a dozen worldwide (or TOP) sponsorships. TOP sponsors have the right to advertise worldwide using the five-ring logo and the designation of "official" sponsor. For example, Coca Cola, which is a TOP sponsor, may advertise anywhere in the world using the famous five-ring Olympic symbol. National sponsors and Games sponsor are restricted to a defined territory. A sponsor of the Rio de Janeiro Olympic Games, for example, may only advertise using the Rio Games logo in the territory of Brazil.

One of the first agreements signed in the Olympic context is the Marketing Plan Agreement. The organizing committee and the IOC meet and make a few overarching decisions regarding structure of the sponsorships. For example, an organizing committee might have three tiers of sponsorships—partner, sponsor, and supplier—each with a different set of rights (the use of the official logos, for example) and benefits (hospitality, accommodations, tickets and so forth). In the Olympic World, a Games organizing committee must extend to all TOP sponsors the benefits and rights given to the sponsors in its top tier. FIFA, the world's most prominent soccer organization, also sells sponsorships at the highest level. The NBA, Major League Baseball, and National Football League all have official sponsors. Sponsorships are also sold by teams (for example, the US Olympic Team, the Dallas Cowboys, and Manchester United). In addition, individual athletes also endorse or sponsor products and brands.

Athletes that have individual contracts with sponsors to wear their clothes or use their equipment when performing can run into problems when competing in the Olympics and in other contexts. The Olympics, as noted, has a rule called "clean venue"—no advertising is allowed in any of the Olympic venues. Exceptions are made for the manufacturers of official apparel. The manufacturer's logo may be shown on the apparel, but restrictions in size and placement apply. The problem arises with athletes who have contractual arrangements with manufacturers other than the official manufacturers. For example, an American NBA star may have an endorsement deal with Nike, but the United States National Team wears Adidas jerseys. This discrepancy would have to be addressed. An interesting example occurred in 2000, at the Sydney Games, when an Australian athlete won the gold medal but was required to throw a towel over the logo on his jersey while standing on the podium. At the Super Games, mentioned above, Shaquille O'Neal was handed a cup bearing the logo of a famous beverage company. The problem was that Shaq had an endorsement deal with the company's competitor. He dropped the cup and stepped away before anyone could take his picture. He then made sure that none of the offending cups were in his proximity for the rest of the game.

Legal Issues Surrounding Broadcasting

Broadcasting is the most financially important commercial part of any Olympic Games—broadcasting revenue dwarfs the revenue from all the other commercial areas. This is true in all sports, where broadcasting is feasible. The structure of the agreement is a license. The top organizing body—the IOC, for example—licenses the right to broadcast the Games in a certain territory to a television network (or, in the case of Japan, a consortium made up of many broadcasters) in that territory, which pays a broadcasting fee. The fee is split between the IOC and the organizing committee, which may have to share its portion with the city and the National Olympic Committee.

The broadcasting agreement contains important territorial restrictions. The modern iteration of the agreement contains provisions about "new media" (Internet and mobile platforms, for example), which present challenges for the IOC and the broadcasters. On the one hand, the IOC is interested in controlling unforeseen media. The broadcasters, on the other hand, want all media, whether now existing or devised in the future, automatically included in the deal. The agreement will also contain a description of the services provided by the IOC (or by the organizing committee in accordance with the terms of an agreement between the IOC and the organizing committee) and certain other matters—for example, space in the international broadcasting center, accreditation, hospitality, accommodations, ticket allotments, and other matters. In most nations in the world, broadcasting is a very politically sensitive area. The right to broadcast freely may sometimes collide with local law. Even the equipment brought in by the broadcasters is heavily monitored.

There are about twenty different broadcasters (including broadcast unions) that receive broadcasting rights for the Olympics. The rights are sold in "quadrennial" segments—four years—including two Olympic Games (a summer and winter Games). The United States is the most expensive, with the price of a single quadrennial approaching a billion dollars. The European Broadcasting Union is the biggest, as it has about seventy countries in it. Japan is probably the third most important. Japan is a consortium comprised of virtually all of Japan's broadcast networks, thus avoiding competitive bidding. An IOC official once told me that Japan is an anathema to the IOC. Other territories include Asia Pacific, Korea, Canada, New Zealand, Australia, and South Africa.

Legal Issues Surrounding the Ceremonies

Stating the obvious, all sporting events are entertainment. Thus, it is not surprising that in major ways the lawyering of a commercial sporting event, especially where broadcasting is involved, involves a facility in entertainment law principles—copyright, publicity rights, and a body of rights applicable in Europe, Japan and other civil law jurisdictions. A lawyer working on the opening and closing ceremonies, for example, must create a body of entertainment contracts (with writers, designers, choreographers, performers, dancers and so forth) that accomplishes critical objectives:

1. The copyright inherent in the creative services of all contributors must in some way be owned or controlled for a very long time by the organizing committee and ultimately by the IOC;
2. All persons filmed or depicted in the broadcast must release the organizing committee of any liability arising from the use of the person's name and likeness in such context;
3. The organizers (and later the IOC) must have the right to freely edit the material created for such ceremonies; and
4. All of these rights and waivers and releases must be assignable to the IOC. It is a massive undertaking full of twists and turns. For example, in Beijing, one of the composers refused to give up the copyright to the composition he was hired to compose. After negotiation, the deal was structured as an exclusive license to the organizing committee (fully sub-licensable to the IOC) with restrictions going forward on the composer's ability to grant licenses to non-Olympic sponsors, for example—the fear of ambush marketing being ever presence in the sports context.

Conclusion

The Olympics is a massive undertaking that requires seven years of planning, preparation, and execution. Lawyers play a vital role in many aspects of this process. They lay the groundwork for protection and actively assist in the enforcement of rights. At the conclusion, the organizing committee will be involved in the process of assigning all intellectual property rights (i.e., trademarks, copyrights and other proprietary material) to the IOC. The organizing committee will work with the IOC on legacy matter—i.e., the use of the Olympic marks on memorials and in venues that housed the various sporting events. Then the organizing committee will dissolve and all eyes will turn to the next Olympic Games.

Aside from the pomp and glory is the commercial reality of the Games. A summer Games has the potential of generating multiple billions in revenues. This reality is not lost on the organizers of the Games or the IOC. Indeed, the governing boards at the top of all sports organizations—

be it of the NBA, MLB, or the IOC—focus on these commercial areas. Much effort goes into the sale of tickets, licensed merchandise, sponsorships, and of course, the lucrative area of broadcasting. Money is a "scorecard" of sorts, because it ensures the continuation of the endeavor—the personal heroics of the athletes, the close finishes, national pride, and the fun of sports.

A sports lawyer understands both of these crucial legal areas—a thorough understanding of intellectual property law and a well-grounded knowledge of how money is made.

Key Takeaways

- Sports law is essentially made up of five areas—entertainment and the four prongs of commerce: ticketing, licensing, sponsorships, and broadcasting. The ultimate objective of professional sports is to entertain—which, in turn, allows people to either buy tickets to go see the event in person or sit in front of their television and watch it, and buy paraphernalia that is branded with the logos and other symbols of the teams they like.
- Entertainment law relates to the pageantry of sport—the opening and closing ceremonies, performers at half time or during the seventh-inning stretch. Contracts with creative personnel and crew must provide for a grant of ownership rights (or at least a durable license) to the organizer and must release the organizer from liabilities related to the use of the person's name and/or likeness. All rights must be cleared.
- Each area of commerce has its own body of rules and laws that need to be taken into consideration by the attorneys involved. Ticketing involves the sale of a license to enter a sporting venue and take a seat. Privacy laws have become important in this process, as the internationalization of sports has evolved. The ticket is a contract, reflecting many of the concerns of the organizers. Licensing and sponsorships are based in the good will associated with the name and trademark of the sports organization—often built up over a long period of time. Lawyers must understand trademark law, licensing, and the rights and obligations of the parties to these agreements. Lawyers must also

become knowledgeable about "ambush marketing" concerns to assist the organizers in thwarting the efforts of non-sponsors. Broadcasting, the most lucrative of the commercial areas, involves an understanding of the rights being licensed and the nature of the services being offered.

- In each of these areas, there are certain customary norms that all lawyers working in sports should strive to understand.

Kelly Charles Crabb is a partner in the Media, Entertainment and Technology Group with Sheppard Mullin Richter & Hampton LLP and is resident in the firm's Los Angeles office. Mr. Crabb's practice emphasizes clients with an entertainment, sports, and media focus and includes a mix of sophisticated and complex financing, production, and content work for substantial U.S., Asian, and European companies. His practice areas include motion pictures, television, Internet, video games, print publishing and other content production, financing, distribution and exhibition; music business contracts; commercial endorsements and advertising; live events (including Olympic Games and other international sporting events, concerts, and stage productions); content rights acquisition and licensing; corporate mergers and acquisitions and joint venture transactions; and matters related to the entertainment and music performance guilds. His book, The Movie Business, which was published by Simon & Schuster in 2005, is regarded as a major work in the filmed entertainment community worldwide.

Mr. Crabb is well known in the Olympic Movement, having performed services related to four Olympic Games. He is currently working on projects for the Rio 2016 Olympic Committee and previously worked on the broadcasting agreement for the London Organizing Committee of the Olympic Games (2012) and entertainment projects for the Salt Lake Olympic Organizing Committee for the Winter Games of 2002. Mr. Crabb acted as international counsel to the Beijing Olympic Organizing Committee for the XXIX Olympiad in 2008. In one of the top sports news stories of 2004, Mr. Crabb successfully represented an Olympic gymnastics champion in connection with a dispute arising at the Athens Games before the Court of Arbitration for Sport, in Lausanne, Switzerland. In other sports-related work, he performed professional services for NBA China and Major League Baseball in China.

Mr. Crabb received his law degree from Columbia University School of Law in 1984, where he was an editor of the Columbia Law Review from 1982-1984. He received his Master's in Public Administration in 1973 and his undergraduate degree in 1971 from

Brigham Young University. Mr. Crabb is a frequent lecturer on entertainment and sports law and a recognized author. Mr. Crabb was selected by the Los Angeles Chapter of the J. Reuben Clark Law Society as "Outstanding Lawyer of 2005." He is a member of both the California and New York state bars.

Intellectual Property Rights in Image Advertising

Jonathan D. Goins

Partner

Lewis Brisbois Bisgaard & Smith LLP

ASPATORE

Introduction

Sports law has long embodied principles of intellectual property rights—both with respect to corporations marketing their trademark brands in advertising sponsorships at major sporting events, and as to athletes lending their fame and notoriety in endorsements. Oftentimes these corporate and individual interests in brand and image advertising are aligned,[1] but when they are not, both sides can become litigious. The typical argument from each side is as follows: athletes have the "right of publicity" to prohibit commercial uses of their name, image, and likeness without permission, but corporations have the "freedom of speech" to communicate their advertising message in a non-commercial manner under the First Amendment.

Athletes (and entertainers and celebrities in general) scored a recent victory recently in this litigious contest over "image advertising" in light of the Seventh Circuit's decision in *Jordan v. Jewel Food Stores*, which reversed a lower court's ruling that Jewel Food Stores' *Sports Illustrated* advertisement featuring a pair of number 23 Jordan basketball shoes was protected under the First Amendment.[2] Before delving further into the "Xs and Os" of Michael Jordan's latest accomplishment, however, it is important to understand the historical development of this "right" of publicity.

The Right of Publicity

The right of publicity is a cause of action available in state court regarding the right of an individual to control the commercial use of his or her

---

[1] Indeed, on April 29, 2014, the National Basketball Association's Commissioner, Adam Silver, announced a lifetime ban against Donald Sterling, owner of the Los Angeles Clippers, for racially insensitive audiotaped comments. A media frenzy of pressure from both player athletes and corporations certainly aided in Mr. Silver's swift and stern pronouncement. In just two days, sixteen corporate sponsors suspended or cancelled their advertising and marketing deals with the Clippers, including CarMax, State Farm, Virgin America, Red Bull, Aquahydrate, Amtrak, Chumash Casino Resort, Lumber Liquidators, Yokohama Tire Company, Corona/Constellation Brands, Samsung, Sprint, Mercedes-Benz, adidas, Burger King and MGM Resorts. *See, e.g.*, Ira Boudway, *Corporate Sponsors End Ties to the Clippers*, BLOOMBERG BUSINESS WEEK, Apr. 28, 2014, available at http://www.businessweek.com/articles/2014-04-28/donald-sterling-and-the-lost-l-dot-a-dot-clippers-sponsors#p1.

[2] *Jordan v. Jewel Food Stores, Inc. (Jordan I)*, 851 F. Supp. 2d 1102 (N.D. Ill. 2012), *rev'd, Jordan v. Jewel Food Stores, Inc., (Jordan II)*, 743 F.3d 509 (7th Cir. 2014).

identity.[3] The earliest case acknowledging this distinct and personal privilege termed as a "right of publicity" was in 1953.[4] The principle is rooted in the cognizable property interest of a person's right against unauthorized commercial uses of his or her name, image, or likeness.[5] Some states expand the right not only to one's name, image, or likeness, but also one's voice, signature, photograph, gestures, distinctive appearances, and mannerisms.[6] The very core of this right of publicity is best articulated by trademark law's most renowned expert, J. Thomas McCarthy:

> The right of publicity is the inherent right of every human being to control the commercial use of his or her identity. This legal right is infringed by unpermitted use which will likely damage the commercial value of this inherent right of human identity and which is not immunized by principles of free speech and free press. Infringement of the right of publicity is a commercial tort, and a form of unfair competition. The right of publicity is property, and is properly categorized as a form of intellectual property.[7]

To expand on McCarthy's syncretic explanation, embedded in sports law is the brand marketing of intellectual property, which popular athletes (and entertainers) have individualized over the past several decades through rights of publicity claims under state law and false endorsement claims under federal trademark law.

Only thirty-one states recognize a right of publicity.[8] As such, athletes' ability to enforce a right of publicity claim can be fairly limited, both jurisdictionally as to where a potential accuser of unauthorized activity can be sued, and substantively as to what relief can be afforded, as not all states recognize monetary damages or attorneys' fees to the prevailing party.

---

[3] RESTATEMENT (THIRD) OF UNFAIR COMPETITION § 46 (1995).
[4] *Haelan Labs., Inc. v. Topps Chewing Gum, Inc.*, 202 F.2d 866 (2d Cir. 1953).
[5] *Zacchini v. Scripps-Howard Broad. Co.*, 433 U.S. 562, 573 (1977).
[6] IND. CODE ANN. §§ 32-36-1 *et seq.* (West).
[7] J. Thomas McCarthy, 5 MCCARTHY ON TRADEMARKS AND UNFAIR COMPETITION § 28:1 (Thomson Reuters 4th ed. 2014).
[8] J. Thomas McCarthy, THE RIGHTS OF PUBLICITY AND PRIVACY 2d § 6:3 (Thomson Reuters 2d ed. 2014).

Trademark Law's False Endorsement Claim

Given some of the limitations of a rights of publicity claim, many athletes such as Kareem Abdul-Jabbar,[9] Jim Brown,[10] Michael Jordan, and Tiger Woods[11] have sought broader protection of their right of publicity through a complementary cause of action called a "false endorsement" claim under federal trademark law (or more specifically under Section 43 of the Lanham Act).[12] Federal trademark law extends to protection of an athlete's name if it is used as a trademark on or in connection with a good or service in commerce. Under Section 43(a) of the Lanham Act, false endorsement occurs when an athlete's identity is connected with a product or service in such a way that consumers are likely to be misled about that athlete's sponsorship or approval of the product or service.[13]

Although securing a federal trademark registration is not a prerequisite for filing suit on a Section 43 claim, there are numerous benefits. Once an athlete's name is secured as a federally registered trademark, the law:

- Grants constructive notice to the public regarding the use of his trademark;
- Creates a presumption of validity of ownership and exclusivity of said use;
- Assists in creating federal jurisdiction when suing in any district court; and
- Provides for greater enhancement of injunctive relief, treble damages, and attorneys' fees.[14]

This explains the recent trend of athletes registering their names, logos, and catch phrases as trademarks with the US Patent & Trademark

[9] *See, e.g., Abdul-Jabbar v. Gen. Motors Corp.*, 85 F.3d 407 (9th Cir. 1996).
[10] *See, e.g., Brown v. Elec. Arts, Inc.*, 724 F.3d 1235 (9th Cir. 2013).
[11] According to the Trademark Electronic Search System, approximately 36 applications incorporate TIGER WOODS or a similar variation thereof as a trademark. *See, e.g., ETW Corp. v. Jireh Publishing, Inc.*, 332 F.3d 915 (6th Cir. 2003).
[12] Lanham Act, 15 U.S.C. § 1125(a) (West); *see, e.g., Parks v. LaFace Records*, 329 F.3d 437, 459 (6th Cir. 2003) ("[C]ourts routinely recognize a property right in celebrity identity akin to that of a trademark holder under § 43(a) [of the Lanham Act]").
[13] Lanham Act, 15 U.S.C. § 1125(a).
[14] 15 U.S.C. §§ 1072, 1111, 1114, 1115 (West).

Office.[15] Indeed, even Johnny Manzeil has adopted his "Johnny Football" and "the house that Johnny built" coined names with several applications for educational and entertainment services, athletic clothing merchandise, and footballs.[16]

The Jordan Case

Expanding on athletic image advertising and claims involving rights of publicity or false endorsement, the Seventh Circuit's *Jordan v. Jewel Food Stores* decision is illustrative. After Jordan was inducted into the [Basketball] Hall of Fame in September 2009, media giant Time, Inc. decided to publish a *Sports Illustrated* commemorative issue acknowledging Jordan's contributions to the game (no surprise there).[17] In soliciting for page ad sponsors, proposals asked for "some play on words or design that is specific to Michael Jordan."[18] One of those ad proposals came from Jewel Food Stores (better known as Jewel-Osco), which operates about 175 grocery stores in the greater Chicago area.[19] Jewel Food's internal copywriter created a message, and its marketing vendor designed the graphics.[20] Jewel Food's ad featured a pair of basketball shoes spotlighted on the hardwood floor of a basketball court. The number twenty-three appears on the tongue of each shoe, with the following message positioned above:

> A Shoe In! After six NBA championships, scores of rewritten record books and numerous buzzer beaters, Michael Jordan's elevation in the Basketball Hall of Fame was never in doubt! Jewel-Osco salutes #23 on his many accomplishments as we honor a fellow Chicagoan who was "just around the corner" for so many years.[21]

---

[15] *See, e.g.*, Kate Thomas, *Sports Stars Seek Profit in Catchphrases*, N.Y. TIMES, Dec. 9, 2010; Brett H. Pavony & Jaia Thomas, *For the Love of the Name: Professional Athletes Seek Trademark Protection*, 2 PACE. INTELL. PROP. SPORTS & ENT. L.F. 153 (2012), *available at* http://digitalcommons.pace.edu/pipself/vol2/iss1/7.
[16] *See* U.S. Trademark Application Serial Nos. 85/839,336; 86/153,461 and 86/178,965.
[17] *Jordan I, supra* 851 F. Supp. 2d at 1104.
[18] *Id.* at 1104.
[19] *Id.*
[20] *Id.*
[21] *Id.*

Beneath the ad message is Jewel-Osco's own registered trademark logo with the slogan: "Good things are just around the corner." A photo of the ad is displayed as Appendix B.

Not pleased with the congratulatory message, Jordan sued the grocery store, claiming $5 million in damages for using his image and likeness in the ad without his permission. Jordan sued on claims of a right of publicity under Illinois state law, and false endorsement under Section 43(a) of federal trademark law.[22]

After summary judgment briefings filed by both parties, a district court judge was faced with deciding whether Jewel Food made commercial use of Jordan's identity for a profit without his permission. These types of claims often turn on whether the messenger engaged in commercial versus non-commercial speech. In simplest terms, if Jewel Food's ad is not commercial in nature, then it is not liable (and vice versa). Factors weighing this proposition involve:

1. Whether the speech is an advertisement;
2. Whether the speech refers to a specific product or service; and
3. Whether the speech has an economic or for-profit motivation.

Ultimately, the district court judge concluded that Jewel Food's ad was not commercial speech, and thus not liable to Jordan's right of publicity claim under the First Amendment. The judge found that the ad's focal message recounted some of Jordan's accomplishments and congratulated him on his career and induction into the Hall of Fame. The judge pointed out that the shoes, the number 23, and the hardwood floor evoke Jordan and the sport and team for which he enjoyed his principal success. According to the judge, at the most basic level, the page does not propose any kind of commercial message, as readers would be at a loss to explain what they have been invited to buy.[23]

As I have opined in previous articles and lectures,[24] the readers would be at a loss to explain why such advertising was not an endorsement, at least at

---

[22] *See* Illinois Right of Publicity Act, 765 ILCS 1075/1 *et seq.*; Lanham Act, 15 U.S.C. § 1125(a).

[23] *Jordan I*, 851 F. Supp. 2d at 1106-07.

[24] *Jordan v. Jewel Food Stores, Inc.: Do the Shoes Make the Man?*, 21 SPORTS MARKETING Q. J. 253 (2012).

the summary judgment stage which requires proof only as to a genuine issue of material fact—such as the shoes (which look like a pair of Jordan shoes), use of the number 23, and a basketball court. At the very least, the ad seems to create a consumer perception of association between Jewel Food and the Jordan brand, whose net worth is over $530 million.[25] There is a legitimate debate as to whether Jewel Food's ad misled the public into thinking that there was some association with Jordan; that it was sponsored, approved, or otherwise endorsed by Jordan himself.

On appeal, the Seventh Circuit reversed the district court's ruling. In doing so, it held that: "Jewel's ad prominently features the Jewel–Osco logo and marketing slogan, which are creatively and conspicuously linked to Jordan in the text of the ad's congratulatory message. Based on its content and context, the ad is properly classified as a form of *image advertising* aimed at promoting the Jewel-Osco brand."[26]

The Circuit defined image advertising as a "form of advertising featur[ing] appealing images and subtle messages alongside the advertiser's brand name or logo with the aim of linking the advertiser to a particular person, value, or idea in order to build goodwill for the brand."[27]

In other words, by congratulating Jordan on his induction into the Hall of Fame seems reasonable, but "considered in context, and without the rose-colored glasses, Jewel's ad has an unmistakable commercial function: enhancing the Jewel-Osco brand in the minds of consumers. This commercial message is implicit but easily inferred, and is the dominant one."[28]

The Circuit reasoned that the ad was considered a form of "image advertising" aimed at promoting goodwill for the Jewel-Osco brand by exploiting public affection for Jordan at an auspicious moment in his career.[29] The case was remanded back to the district court.

---

[25] *See* FORBES, *America's Richest Athletes* (Sept. 21, 2011); FORBES, *The World's Top Sports Brands* (Feb. 3, 2010).
[26] *Jordan II*, 743 F.3d at 512.
[27] *Id.* at 520.
[28] *Jordan II*, 743 F.3d at 518.
[29] *Id.* at 519.

Key Takeaways

The *Jordan* case provides a few key takeaways for consideration. The most glaring implication is that the decision keeps alive the viability of a claim for misappropriation of image advertising—not just for athletes, but also entertainers and celebrities.[30] Other takeaways include as follows:

- *Indemnify.* For corporations involved in advertising sponsorships with other parties, you want to ensure that the events' holder (i.e., NFL for Super Bowl) is on the hook for any legal claims from third parties, such as athletes, for any ads incorporating unauthorized names, likeness, and images subject to a right of publicity claim. This is often referred to as an indemnification clause. Make sure this is clear and in writing on the front end, before you begin creating the ad or design relating to the ad. The same is true for created trademarks or copyrights; do not make any admission or representation that what you created for the company is free and clear of any rights of others involving potential infringement.
- *Ad Clearance.* For corporations issuing their own advertising, ensure that you or your lawyers are reviewing advertisements for logos and other taglines worthy of copyright or trademark protection. Equally important is clearing any advertisements to ensure that you are not using anyone else's copyright or trademark. Many copyright holders are monitoring to see if others are using photos taken from Internet search engines without permission. Just because you can copy and paste an image does not mean you can use the image without paying for it. Also, be mindful of the Federal Trade Commission's endorsement guidelines, which provide direction as to how your athletes and other talent should properly offer endorsements and testimonials.
- *Police.* Navigating through corporate and athletes' brand and image advertising is a delicate balance, especially in today's fragmented, social media driven environment. The rapid proliferation of digital new media technology has significantly increased corporate

[30] *Id.* at 520 ("A contrary holding would have sweeping and troublesome implications for athletes, actors, celebrities, and other trademark holders seeking to protect the use of their identities or marks.").

advertising in the sports industry. In fact, sports advertisers increased mobile Internet advertising by 411 percent in 2013, with an estimated worldwide spending of $29.43 billion in 2014.[31] Traditionally, a corporation could advertise with one of the four major networks involving one of the three major professional sports leagues (NFL, NBA, or MLB) and feel assured that its brand advertising and message was widely disseminated to a broad audience. In today's era, there are dozens and dozens of networks offering unique online programming content, more sports enthusiasts following sports beyond the major three leagues, and ambush marketing tactics being employed by corporate competitors not otherwise sponsoring certain sports advertising events. This requires more corporate spending, but also more vigilance in ensuring you are not infringing on third party intellectual property rights. For sports and talent marketing agencies representing athletes, ensure that you are routinely monitoring the Internet and related mediums for unauthorized name, image, and likeness in advertising. They are relying on you to police and protect their brand, beyond just developing commercial magnetism and marketing value for additional revenue streams off the field. Now more than ever, athletes and celebrities are faced with enormous concerns regarding appropriate commercial use of their images.

- *Keep Filing Trademarks*. For athletes, ensure that you are evaluating whether to seek federal trademark registration for your names, catchphrases, or the like, in connection with entertainment-related services such as endorsements. As explained above, trademarking an athlete's name has enormous benefits and can be a nice "one-two punch" with a right of publicity claim. Securing a federal trademark of an athlete's name creates a presumption that you own and possess the exclusive right to use your name nationwide on or in connection with the service or product as listed in your registration—that you own what you claim to own, in other words. Having a federal trademark registration also creates automatic standing in federal court and potentially avoids jurisdictional issues when faced with concerns over commercial misappropriation and unauthorized use of

[31] eMarketer, *Across Industries, Mobile Ad Spend Increases Dramatically*, Jan. 2, 2014, *available at* http://www.emarketer.com/Article/Across-Industries-Mobile-Ad-Spend-Increases-dramatically/1010499#sthash.NQj0sKJL.dpuf.

an athlete's name, likeness, and image. It also provides for significant monetary damages if found liable for having copied or misappropriated one's trademark. Finally, trademarks are intangible intellectual property assets worth a lot of money. One can seek royalties or fees through trademark licenses. One can also pledge trademarks as collateral in corporate transactions. So it makes dollars and "sense" as to why Jordan has over thirty federal trademark applications or registrations for his name in connection with cologne, after shave, sports bags, sportswear, underwear, restaurants, golf club services, and endorsements.

- *Play Defense.* For corporations or marketing agencies seeking to employ aggressive marketing tactics, ensure that you are evaluating the defenses of fair use, non-trademark use, or First Amendment non-commercial speech.

Jonathan D. Goins is a partner with Lewis Brisbois Bisgaard & Smith LLP, one of the nation's largest law firms. Mr. Goins is an intellectual property attorney practicing in copyright and trademark-related transactions and litigation with an industry focus in entertainment and sports. He is a frequent speaker and author on intellectual property, and lectures on copyright and trademark law as an adjunct professor at Atlanta's John Marshall Law School.

APPENDICES

Appendix A: Harassment Investigation Checklist 138

Appendix B: Jewel-Osco Advertisement at Issue in *Jordan v. Jewel Food Stores* 154

APPENDIX A

HARASSMENT INVESTIGATION CHECKLIST

The following checklist and interview forms are provided to help you conduct a thorough investigation into any harassment complaint.

- ☐ Consider the order in which all of the investigation interviews will be conducted.

  - Complainant.
  - Alleged harasser.
  - Co-workers and other witnesses.
  - Second interview of the Complainant to discuss any factual questions as a result of the investigation.
  - Second interview with the alleged harasser to discuss any factual questions as a result of the investigation.

- ☐ Interview each witness separately in an office or room where the discussion will not be overheard by other witnesses, the alleged harasser, or any other unauthorized persons.

  - Two managers should participate in the interview process. At least one of the investigating managers should be thoroughly familiar with harassment law and the Company's harassment policies and procedures. One manager should be designated as the interviewer, and the other should act primarily as a witness and take notes of the discussion.
  - Before beginning the interview, explain the purpose of the interview by referring generally to recent complaints about the relationship between the Complainant and the alleged harasser. Do not necessarily discuss the issue of harassment, so that you do not taint the witness's recollection of the events.
  - Emphasize that the Company takes these charges very seriously and that the Company is investigating these charges by interviewing all potential witnesses in compliance with Company policy.

- Explain that upon completion of the investigation, the Company will attempt to determine what occurred, and will take appropriate action based on its determination.
- Both the alleged victim and the alleged harasser should be advised that each will be apprised of the results of the investigation and any action taken.
- Instruct each witness interviewed not to discuss the matters covered during the interview with any co-employee or the alleged harasser.
- Explain to the witness that confidentiality is necessary to protect the integrity of the investigation and to ensure that the Company receives trustworthy information in an atmosphere free from coercion.
- Avoid leading questions.
- Ask open ended, non-judgmental questions. Use investigation interview forms where appropriate.
- Explain to all witnesses that retaliation will not be tolerated.

☐ Avoid the appearance of impropriety or favoritism in conducting interviews.
☐ Observe and record all physical and verbal reactions of witnesses.
☐ Do not record conclusions regarding credibility.
☐ Avoid judgmental statements or furthering of myths or stereotypes.
☐ Interview all possible witnesses:

Complainant.

- Alleged harasser.
- Complainant's supervisor.
- Alleged harasser's supervisor.
- Co-workers.
- Other:

____

☐ Review Complainant's personnel file.
☐ Review alleged harasser's personnel file.

- ☐ Discuss investigation results and proposed action with investigation team. This discussion should be limited to those with a need to know the results of the investigation, such as the Complainant's supervisor, the alleged harasser's supervisor, and senior Human Resources Department staff.
- ☐ Consider credibility determinations. Factors include:

  - Memory.
  - Perception.
  - Veracity (truthfulness).
  - Corroboration or lack of corroboration, and implications of such determination.
  - Bias of witnesses.
  - Consistency of accounts.
  - Prior misconduct or lack thereof, and implications of such misconduct.
  - Plausibility of accounts.

- ☐ Review any documentary evidence.
- ☐ Consider appropriate remedial action:

  - Document investigation in personnel file.
  - Verbal warning.
  - Written warning.
  - Suspension.
  - Demotion.
  - Termination.

- ☐ Factors in determining appropriate remedial action.

  - Credibility determinations.
  - Prior conduct, if any.
  - Prior discipline of alleged harasser.
  - Level of harassment, including type and frequency of conduct.
  - Alleged harasser's knowledge of Company rules of conduct.

- Prior disciplinary "precedent" for identical, similar or analogous misconduct.
- Political considerations within the organization.
- Public and employee relations issues.
- Other:

  ____

☐ Review harassment investigation and findings.

- Was the Company harassment policy adequate?
- Were the employees aware of the terms of the harassment policy.
- Was the harassment complaint procedure adequate?
- Did the investigator uncover other issues which need to be addressed?
- Other:

  ____

☐ Implement changes to harassment policies and procedures where appropriate.

Interviewer: ____________________________ Date: ________________
Witness: ____________________________ Date: ________________

Complainant Interview Form

Name: ______________________________ Date: ______________

Position: ______________________ Supervisor: ________________

- ☐ Name and position of the alleged harasser:

  ____

- ☐ Date and time of the harassment: _______________________
- ☐ Did the harassment occur more than once? Yes _____ No ______
  If so, how often did it occur? ____________________________
  If it occurred more than once, on what dates and at what times did it take place? ____
- ☐ For each incident, ascertain and document what occurred. Try to get as many details as possible, even though this may be uncomfortable for the complainant. Use additional pages if necessary. Ask open ended, non-judgmental questions, such as:

  - Did the alleged harasser touch the Complainant?

    ____

  - If so, where was the Complainant touched?

    ____

  - Was the Complainant touched more than once?
    Yes _____ No ______
  - Did the alleged harasser threaten the Complainant in any way?

    ____

  - If so, what was the threat or threats?

    ____

  - How long was the incident, for example a few seconds, five minutes? ____

    ____

  - Where did the incidents of harassment take place?

    ____

    ____

  - Were there any witnesses to the incidents of harassment? If so, who were the witnesses? ____________________________

    ____

- Does the Complainant know of any others subjected to the same behavior?

  ____

  ____

- Does the Complainant know motive for harassment?

  ____

- How did the Complainant respond to the harassment? Did he or she make any effort to bring it to a halt?

  ____

- Did the Complainant tell anyone else about the incidents of harassment: superiors, co-workers, family, friends, government representatives, attorneys? If so, get details concerning who, what, when, where and the response, if any.

  ____

  ____

- Does the Complainant have any tangible evidence or records of harassment: notes, letters or memos to or from harasser, witnesses; calendar or diary entries, memos, letters, notes etc. by Complainant; tape recordings, surreptitious or otherwise; formal complaint forms to any agencies?

  ____

  ____

- How did the Complainant feel about the harassment at the time it occurred? ______________________________

  ____

- Does the Complainant feel the same way now? If not, what is different about how the Complainant now feels, and what brought about the difference? ____________________

  ____

- Does the alleged harasser have control over the compensation, working conditions or future employment of the Complainant?

  ____

  ____

- Has the alleged harasser made or carried out any threats or promises in connection with the alleged sexual harassment?

  ____

  ____

Does the Complainant know or suspect there are other victims of harassment by the same person? If so, who are they?

____

____

- To what extent were others in control made aware of the situation? ______________________________________

____

☐ What action would the Complainant like to have taken?

____

____

☐ Ask the employee to write and sign a detailed description of all events to support the harassment claim.

Interviewer: ______________________ Date: ____________
Witness: ______________________ Date: ____________

Alleged Harasser Interview Form

Name: ______________________________ Date: ________________

Position: ________________________ Supervisor: ________________

- ☐ Prepare for the investigation meeting with the alleged harasser. This meeting should take place in private, although the company should have two representatives present. The investigator should outline the allegations in advance to ensure that all subjects are discussed.
- ☐ Provide the alleged harasser with a copy of the company policy, emphasizing the employer's commitment to enforcing the policy. This step should be followed even if it is suspected that the allegations are not true.
- ☐ Answer the alleged harasser's pre-interview concerns and suspicions about the investigation.
- ☐ Advise the alleged harasser generally about the investigation and strict policies of confidentiality and avoidance of retaliation.
- ☐ Ask direct and detailed questions based on information provided by all witnesses, such as:

  - Were the alleged harasser and complainant working together on the date(s) complainant say harassment occurred?

    ____

    ____

  - Does the alleged harasser recall any interaction with complainant on those dates? If so, what was the context of the interaction?

    ____

  - Were there any witnesses present? ________________________
  - What was the substance of any conversation between the complainant and alleged harasser?

    ____

- ☐ Expect an adamant denial. For each denial, request that the harasser identify corroborating witnesses or evidence, and detail any "alibi."
- ☐ If the alleged harasser acknowledges any conduct, ascertain and document what occurred. Try to get as many details as possible, even though this may be uncomfortable for the alleged harasser.

☐ Use additional pages if necessary. Ask open ended, non-judgmental questions, such as:

- Did the alleged harasser touch the Complainant? ___________
- If so, where was the Complainant touched? _______________
- Was the Complainant touched more than once? ____________
- Was the touching done at the direction of the Complainant or the alleged harasser? ________________________________

  ____
- Did the alleged harasser threaten the Complainant in any way?

  ____

  ____
- If so, what was the threat or threats?

  ____

  ____
- How long was the incident, for example a few seconds, five minutes? ____
- Where did the incident take place?

  ____
- Were there any witnesses to the incident? If so, who were the witnesses? ___________________________________

  ____
- How did the Complainant respond to the incident? Did he or she make any effort to bring it to a halt?

  ____
- How did the alleged harasser feel about the incident at the time it occurred? ___________________________________

  ____
- Did the alleged harasser do or say anything that could have been misunderstood or could be intentionally misrepresented?

  ____

☐ Ask the alleged harasser about his/her beliefs or suspicions as to why the reports or complaints have been made (*i.e.*, ulterior motives, prior consensual relationships, retaliation by the complaining employee, attempts at job security in the face of poor performance evaluations).

- Did the Complainant engage in any conduct which the alleged harasser felt was inappropriate or made the alleged harasser feel uncomfortable? ______________________________

  ____

☐ Has the Complainant ever said or done anything that would lead the alleged harasser or others to believe that the complained-of conduct was not "unwelcome?" ______________________________

____

☐ What is the level of supervision between the alleged harasser and the complainant? ______________________________

____

☐ How frequently do the alleged harasser and the complainant work together? ______________________________

☐ Has the alleged harasser been previously accused of harassment?

____

- If so, what were the circumstances?

  ____

  ____

☐ Advise that if the evidence establishes harassment, the company will take appropriate disciplinary action against the alleged harasser and the complainant will be fully informed about the company's determination.

☐ Other:

Interviewer: ______________________________ Date: ______________

Witness: ______________________________ Date: ______________

Co-employee Interview Form

Name: ______________________________ Date: ______________
Position: ________________________ Supervisor: ______________

- ☐ Did the co-worker see any alleged harassing incident?
- ☐ If so, what occurred? Try to get as many details as possible (use additional pages if necessary), asking open ended, non-judgmental questions such as:

  - What happened?

    ____

    ____

  - What was said by the alleged harasser?

    ____

  - Did the alleged harasser touch the Complainant in any way?

    ____

  - When did all of this happen?

    ____

  - Who else was present?

    ____

  - What (if anything) did the Complainant say or do in response to the alleged harasser's conduct?

    ____

    ____

  - Did anyone else say or do anything during the incident?

    ____

    ____

  - Did the co-employee later tell anyone about the incident and if so who did you tell and what was their response?

    ____

    ____

    ____

- ☐ Did the co-employee see more than one alleged harassing incident between the alleged harasser and the Complainant? If so, ask questions such as those on the preceding list for each incident.

☐ Did the Complainant ever discuss the issue of alleged harassment with the co-employee?

- How did the Complainant respond to the harassment?

  ____

  ____

- Did he or she make any effort to bring it to a halt?

  ____

☐ Did the co-worker notice any appreciable change in the Complainant's behavior? ______________________

____

☐ Did the Complainant become more or less emotional, upset, or moody at work, specifically with or near the alleged harasser? Please specify.

____

____

☐ Has the co-employee personally seen or heard of sexual harassment by the alleged harasser against any other Company employees besides the Complainant? If so, try to get as many details about what occurred as possible, asking open ended, non-judgmental questions such as those listed above.

☐ Has the co-employee heard another co-employee speak or complain about sexual harassment by the alleged harasser that the co-employee did not personally witness? If so:

- Who told the co-employee about the alleged harassment?

  ____

- Who was allegedly harassed?

  ____

- What was the form of the alleged harassment?

  ____

- What happened?

  ____

  ____

- When did it happen?

  ____

- Who else was present?

  ____

- What did anyone else allegedly say or do during the incident?

  ____

  ____

- Whom did the co-employee later tell about the incident and what was the response? ______________________________

  ____

- Is there any reason the co-employee can think of why the alleged harasser would have thought that the conduct in question was welcomed?

  ____

  ____

- Does the co-employee know any reason why the Complainant would misrepresent allegations? Why harasser more-likely-than not committed misconduct? ______________________________

  ____

- Who does the co-employee believe (in cases where harasser denies allegations outright)? Why?

  ____

  ____

☐ Is the co-employee aware of any other incidents of sexual harassment by any other Company employees? If so:

- Describe the incident.

  ____

  ____

- Who was involved?

  ____

  ____

- Identify all witnesses.

  ____

  ____

- When did it occur?

  ____

- Was Company management advised about the incident promptly and what was the response?

  ____

  If Company management was not made aware of the incident promptly, why not? ______________________________

  ____

☐ Other:

Interviewer: ______________________________ Date: ______________

Witness: ______________________________ Date: ______________

REACHING A CONCLUSION

After you have interviewed the complainant, the alleged harasser and any relevant witnesses, the following questions will help you reach a conclusion and decide how best to respond to the complainant's allegations.

MEETING WITH THE COMPLAINANT

Consider and discuss the following:

- **What did you discover?**
- **What does the Complainant want as a remedy?**
- **Is this a complaint under your policy?**
- **Is there enough here to begin an investigation?**
- **Is there evidence of sexual harassment?**
- **Should you consider a referral to the Company's Employee Assistance Plan?**
- **Is there a workers' compensation claim involved here? If so, does this change your response to the complaint?**
- **What didn't you learn?**

MEETING WITH THE ALLEGED HARASSER

Consider and discuss the following:

- **What did you discover?**
- **Do you think the alleged harasser's alibi has merit?**
- **What didn't you learn?**
- **What, if anything, is the next step in the investigation process?**

MEETING WITH THE COWORKER/WITNESS

Consider and discuss the following:

- **What did you discover?**
- **Did this change your decision about whose story you believe?**

- **What didn't you learn from this witness?**
- **What, if anything, is the next step in the investigation process?**

FINAL DETERMINATION AND REMEDIAL ACTION

Consider and discuss the following:

- **Which witnesses were credible?**
- **Was sexual harassment committed?**
- **What would be appropriate remedial action?**

  a) Documentation in personnel file.
  b) Verbal warning.
  c) Written warning.
  d) Suspension.
  e) Demotion.
  f) Termination.

- Why was the remedial action chosen?
- Is there anything the Company could do to prevent such harassment claims in the future?
- If so, what?

Courtesy of Donald Prophete, Littler Mendelson

APPENDIX B

JEWEL-OSCO ADVERTISEMENT AT ISSUE IN *JORDAN v. JEWEL FOOD STORES*

Courtesy of Jonathan D. Goins, Lewis Brisbois Bisgaard & Smith LLP

ASPATORE